IT'S NOT ABOUT THE PIE

A Fresh Look at Hospitality

IT'S NOT ABOUT THE PIE

A Fresh Look at Hospitality

NICKI CORINNE WHITE

Carpenter's Son Publishing

Published by Carpenter's Son Publishing, Franklin, Tennessee

Published in association with Larry Carpenter of Christian Book Services, LLC   www.christianbookservices.com

Unless otherwise noted, scripture taken from the NEW AMERICAN STANDARD BIBLE®, Copyright © 1960,1962,1963,1968,1971,1972,1973,1975,1977,1995 by The Lockman Foundation. Used by permission.

Scripture taken from THE HOLY BIBLE, NEW INTERNATIONAL VERSION®, NIV® Copyright © 1973, 1978, 1984, 2011 by Biblica, Inc.™ Used by permission. All rights reserved worldwide.

Cover Design by Jessica Owinyo
Interior Design by Adept Content Solutions
Edited by Adept Content Solutions
Cover and Interior Photographs by Jessica Owinyo, Jamie Hudson, Annie Mintz, Daniel Beighley, Susan Greene, Maureen Loeffler, and Jessica Everett

Printed in the United States of America
Trade Paperback 978-1-949572-03-2
Hardcover 978-1-949572-04-9

hos·pi·tal·i·ty

the friendly and generous reception and entertainment of guests, visitors and strangers.

Synonyms: friendliness, hospitableness, warm reception, welcome, helpfulness, neighborliness, warmth, kindness, congeniality, geniality, cordiality, courtesy, amenability, generosity, entertainment, catering, food

com·pas·sion

sympathetic concern for the sufferings and misfortunes of others

Synonyms: sympathy, empathy, care, concern, solicitude, sensitivity, warmth, love, tenderness, mercy, leniency, tolerance, kindness, humanity, charity

To My Craig

I am dedicating this book on hospitality to my partner in hospitality for the past thirty-four years: my husband, Craig. In a marriage, making your home a welcoming place for all who enter it must be a team effort. You need to be in sync. You may have different ideas or tastes on some things, but together you create your home. And through thick and thin you experience life together. Your home is a respite for both your guests and your family. It gives you a feeling of peace and calm when you walk in. You kick off your shoes, put on your slippers, toss down your purse or backpack, and sink into your favorite sofa or chair. You pat your dog on the head and prop up your feet.

I am very thankful to Craig for putting up with my crazy artistic ideas. There was a time when he would come home from a business trip and would ask what I had changed when he was gone. Had I painted a mural on the wall, repainted the entire downstairs, dug a new flower bed, or redecorated an entire room? It is true that I have done some pretty wild things. He is probably glad I am not as apt to do so much as I was twenty years ago.

I am also grateful that God gave me a person who is so generous. Not only does he allow me to give away anything I wish, but he has also given of his time and resources to many. I would not even be able to write this book on giving to others if he had not been so encouraging through the years.

Thank you so much, sweetheart, for being my partner in crime.

Love you forever,

Nicki

Contents

Acknowledgments

Photographers Jamie Hudson, Annie Mintz, and Jessica Owinyo: This book could not exist without these young women. All this incredible photography astounded me. They are so talented and willing to work hard to make this book happen. I am forever grateful to them.

Jessica Everett: This oldest daughter of mine put days, weeks, and months into this book. At least a couple times a week, we would meet to sort through emails, deadlines, edits. So very thankful for her. She is indispensable.

Nathan White: Wow. We would not have either of our websites without Nathan. And then update after update. I am thankful he is so patient with this process. Thank you, son of mine, for being so willing to work on this!

3:12 Team: Ruthanne Beddoe, Courtney Jordan, Amy Crist, Susan Greene, Re Loeffler, Tori Loeffler, Julie Taddicken, Ashley Taylor, Craig White, and the above people, too! Thank you for coming to all the random meetings, working on crazy projects, and basically being helpful and supportive in this project.

Contributors Dick Barrett, Ruthanne Beddoe, Dan and Lyn Beighley, Patti Boliou, Cathy Chan, Jennifer Frendt, John Gibson, Mardell Gill, Mallory Graftius, Susan Greene, Coral Kenegy, Re Loeffler, Betty Lombardi, Diana Malcolm, Laura Malcolm, Moe Malcolm, Julie Neuneker, Juanita Penn, Paul and Marsha Philbrook, Virginia Schumacher, Lisa Shumaker, Sue Shumaker, and Lisa Wood: These people shared their hearts, lives, décor ideas, and recipes. They are valued beyond measure.

"Nicki's book is a joy to read; it is warm and inviting, just like her home. She reminds us of the importance of ministry, of using all that God has given us to minister His love to others. You will receive a gentle nudge to do what God's word commands us in Romans 12:13, 'practice hospitality.' You will come away ready to host your next, or first, guests. For some of us, it isn't as easy as she makes it seem, but she reminds us *It's Not about the Pie*. It's about the heart."

Patrick and Tonya Ireland, Military Chaplain, US Army; former missionary and military wife

"Nicki has a track record of demonstrating hospitality. Her words are valuable to us, not only because they are needed but because she has put them into practice. Our own personal memories of enjoying her hospitality are precious and I know these wonderful words will inspire others to practice hospitality in new and effective ways. Thanks for sharing your insights and experiences with us all, Nicki."

Pastor Geoff Williams

"Nicki skillfully and creatively encourages each one of us to joyfully embrace the unique space that God has given us and to never underestimate the power of His love shown through the way we share our homes and our lives with others."

Marissa Dickey, Missionary to Colombia, South America

"In this day and age when, with the flick of a finger, Pinterest provides thousands upon thousands of ideas and images, it is easy to become overwhelmed when gathering inspiration to decorate, put on parties or pull together different ways to help others. The desire to be perfect causes me to sometimes freeze and not do anything at all in helping people to feel warm and welcomed because I am measuring myself against what I deem perfection. Nicki's book, It's Not About the Pie, provides warm, sound guidance that hospitality is a mindset and 'that God can use imperfect people to perfectly bless other imperfect people with everyone having a good time in the process.' I relish reading those words as they remind me to relax, be my imperfect self. and show warmth and compassion to everyone God puts in my path."

Sarah Zimik, Chief Development Officer at Boise Rescue Mission Ministries; Co-Owner of Empty Hand Combat; and Co-Founder of International Missionary Network

"Too many of us have grown up thinking that only some people have the gift of hospitality. Nicki is giving that gift to all of us who long to create a home where people feel welcome, loved and valued. She makes is easy to see the heart of hospitality is within reach. Her book is a joyful discovery of how-to's and heart."

Dee Sarton, News Anchor for KTVB News Channel 7

Introduction

*"We think sometimes that poverty is only being hungry,
naked and homeless. The poverty of being unwanted,
unloved and uncared for is the greatest poverty.
We must start in our own homes to
remedy this kind of poverty."*
—Mother Teresa

We've all been there: you walk into her home and are instantly amazed by its refreshing scent. It appears to be without fault in every way. The colors in her interior decorating palette flow beautifully. If you are a creative sort who has been fascinated with decorating, entertaining, and interior decorating from childhood like me, a hundred new decorating ideas you want for your own home pop into your head.

I am an artist. I have always made things for my home and love decorating but I am also a busy person and not a perfectionist. Sometimes my home has that lived-in look—most the time, actually. I would like to think it's my heart-attitude of hospitality, of trying to bless from the heart, that is what I hope everyone feels when they enter my home today. You will notice I use the word *home* and not *house*; a house is just a building, but to my mind, a "home" is a happening, an ongoing place of feeling embraced.

What about my home? Well, I have many interesting items. Maybe I have painted a mural on the wall or made a new floral arrangement, but I have also been busy in the kitchen or studying at the table. People often comment on how much they love my home, but many people have also said to me over the years, "Your house looks so *comfortable*, Nicki." What does that mean, exactly? My house does not always look great. I know I have stacks of stuff here or there and I am always in the middle of a project. My best friend has an amazingly gorgeous home, and I do wish I could always have mine ready for guests. She is an inspiration to me so that I may be able to also have my home ready for people to enter. Proverbs 27:17 says, "Iron sharpens iron." In this case, I'd say that seeing my friend's immaculate, heaven-smelling house motivates me every time I visit and causes me to work on those areas where I am not gifted. I've learned that an immaculate house is not a sometimes thing; you've got to work at it. However, knowing I will never realize perfection, I have to acknowledge that my best efforts at entertaining are going to be "imperfect." Despite this, I intend to entertain with a heart full of love. My aspiration is to have Christian love be what they notice and remember most after a visit! Meanwhile, I still want to serve others and use my home as a welcoming place. This has been a passion of mine for the past thirty years. How can I embrace who I am and the gifts that I have and use them to the fullest? Since we are all gifted in different ways, let us use what we have to welcome others. I love decorating. I love having people over. I love helping others and welcoming people into my home—and not just my friends or family. My aspiration is to be a blessing to anyone who crosses my path who is in a time of need.

The purpose of this book is to try to inspire every reader to entertain others, no matter how opulent or humble your circumstances. Hopefully, it will offer you a few ideas that you can use for entertaining. No matter who we are or what kind of space we live in, we can all share what we have with others because HOSPITALITY is a heart thing.

It's Not About the Pie reflects the concept that things do not have to be perfect to welcome someone into your home. Because it is not about having a fancy home or perfect meal, but about making someone feel loved, cared for, and like they can drop in anytime.

People who know me now may say, "Well, it's easy for you to have people into your home. You have a nice house." I assure you that has not always been the case. I did not grow up in a home where I could have friends over, so I did not learn much about entertaining in that era of my life. After we married, my husband and I started to practice hospitality. I started with the people in my own home. It's a lot easier to entertain when your spouse knows you care about him most of all, and it's a lot easier to get his help, too!

Our newlywed first home was 350 square feet, and we loved to invite people over. Over the years, I have hosted many less than perfect events and have blessed people in good times and in tough times. Everyone likes feeling like they matter, like someone cares about them. One key to my success in entertaining? I learned to adapt using limited resources and to use my space for whatever might be needed. How, you might ask? It's so easy, you won't believe it. Heart costs nothing. Always let everything you do be done with love, and I promise that people will notice and will want to return.

All that love in your heart is going to want some recipes. I have included some of my favorite recipes that I like to use whenever I entertain; most of them have been working for me for decades, so please use, modify, and enjoy them! I've also included some quick-fix ideas for decorating and some tips on how to successfully start opening your home to others. My favorite parts of this book are the places where I will share stories of how others have inspired me in my growth as a Christian woman trying to minister hope and hospitality. They are who I learned from. I've included them so you can also learn from their examples. Ways I have learned to share what I have, even if things aren't optimal. It concerns me when people say they are not "gifted" in hospitality, because I used to feel that way. Here I am now, inadequate me, passing on what I have learned to you. In Titus 2:3–5, the Apostle Paul talked about the importance of older women mentoring younger women and having happy homes. It is my encouragement to use your home to reach out to those around you, one step at a time. It doesn't have to be a holiday party; maybe invite someone over for coffee or tea for starters, and then take it from there.

Each of us has our own journey that grows and shapes us, teaching us how we can best share kindness with others. We should make it a habit to be generous and gracious to others, and to let them know that no matter how late or inconvenient the hour, they can show up at your door and crash for the night, or maybe you can provide a listening ear. Perhaps a neighbor needs the leaves raked or a meal during a time of crisis. There are countless ways to help others. This book will barely scratch the surface, but I hope to inspire you to take a fresh look at hospitality and the many ways you can be welcoming to others.

PART 1

The Big Idea

"Share with the Lord's people who are in need. Practice hospitality."
—Romans 12:13 (NIV)

CHAPTER 1

Hospitality is Giving of Ourselves

*"Hospitality isn't about inviting people into our perfect homes,
it's about inviting them into our imperfect hearts."*
—Edie Wadsworth

When I was growing up, we did not have people come to our home. It was an older home, and our mom did not feel it was ready for guests. As a child, I wanted to be able to have people over. Maybe that is why hospitality has become such an important part of my life today.

When my husband Craig and I first got married, I could not wait to set up our nest. Craig was attending college and working as a manager at Taco Bell to support us. We lived in such a tiny place that there was not much to set up. We had a little garden spot behind our duplex where I attempted a garden, but the ants that infested our backyard devoured it. Next, to make our duplex look homey and cheery, I set flower pots in the front yard; the snails living in the ground cover ivy plantings feasted on them, and my beautiful flowers became barren flower pots filled with dirt and snail slime tracks. Never mind that decorating on the inside was a further exercise in futility, as whenever we got a good rain, runoff water took the shortcut through our bedroom on its way to the sea, soaking everything in its path and even ruining my art supplies, which had been stored in our dresser.

We were deeply in love, and it's a good thing, as reality in that duplex was nothing like what I had dreamed our first home as newlyweds would be.

Although that first house was not optimal, we hosted a few dinners with friends in that little place during those eighteen months. Entertaining in that home was very much like going grocery shopping with limited funds and a long list of items you want. It was challenging, and it forced me to plan and to rely on creativity when the money wasn't optimal.

Entertaining is a mindset; everywhere we moved was like a clean sheet of paper and a new box of crayons. Each new place presented us with new options to entertain, and it was challenging (and fun!) to figure out how to make each new residence a homey place with new issues regarding how to best utilize new spaces, decorate bare walls, and set up each new kitchen. I am so thankful that my husband enjoyed those times of change with me and let me open our home. He didn't have to. He would much rather have alone time with our family. I love those times, too, but something pushed me on. I don't really know why I wanted company so much, but I wanted to create a haven for our family that was sufficient for us to host friends and family, have game nights, and offer a place for neighbor kids to play. To make your home a hub, the key is to be *ready and willing* and to be *open* to the possibilities. Maybe an opportunity will only come once, ever. Take that opportunity.

One of my biggest motivations for this book is how many times I've heard people saying that they'd never have people over because they don't feel their house is very presentable, or maybe they think they aren't gifted with a hostess's knack for hospitality. What's funny is that I usually look at their home and think, "Wow, this is a great place for people. I don't understand." We should not feel let down for not having what we define as "the perfect home" or feel discouraged that our home is not right, but rejoice in what we have and that we can share it with our friends, neighbors, and family.

Simply put, hospitality is making people feel welcome in your home or at the social event you are hosting.

My dear friend from college, Re, shared a story about her friend, Monalta, who is such a gracious person. She is very community-minded and loves to draw people from the same

community together. Their children are about the same age, and a few of them went to high school together. A few times on the first day of school, Monalta hosted a get-together for some of the moms. They met for a short time and had tea or coffee and a few goodies some of the ladies brought. It was great—simple and great. Who thought to do that? Monalta did.

There are eighty-eight keys on a piano keyboard, and there must be at least that many ways to *give* to people, including opening your home, welcoming new neighbors, inviting church guests out for a meal or a dinner at your home, or taking food to a family suffering a protracted illness, unemployment, or even a death. Everybody loves getting Christmas cookies, and delivering a tray is a great way to show someone you care. Other ideas could be driving a shut-in to a medical or hair appointment, taking care of someone's kids while the parent takes a much-needed nap or has a date night, or even just raking leaves or shoveling snow for a neighbor who might be widowed or disabled. Your opportunities to be a blessing are limited only by you. Such acts of generosity show your love and care for others; it is a way of imitating Christ [He fed the 5,000, remember?] It is essential to make it plain that they owe you nothing and do not have to reciprocate. To give freely means not to expect anything in return. An example of this is when my friend, Melanie, watched my four kids for me one day. Her kids were older, so she did not need me to watch hers. I felt guilty. Then she said, "Just do the same for someone else sometime." This was a great example to me as a young mom. Even though she was my age, she was willing to help me, even when I didn't understand her selfless act at that time. I could not return this favor to her, but I could learn from it, remember it, and do the same for someone else when I could.

Hospitality became such a huge part of my mindset that I find myself wanting to welcome others even if my home is not at its best. I think the key is that I don't want to worry about the mess at eleven at night while a hurting someone needs to share their heart. Does that mean I don't care about the mess and I don't work at making my house ready? No. I get concerned if I have a pile of laundry or dishes in the sink, but I will not shut someone out if they need me. Taking time despite my house looking too "casual" also involves taking time for my family, too. I want my home to be a haven for my family also, and I pray to God that I always make them feel more important to me than a sink full of dishes or laundry piled in the hallway.

Last year, I attended a ladies' retreat, and the speaker shared her heart regarding hospitality. One of the things that spoke to me was that she had made a map of her neighborhood. Every time she met a neighbor, she would go inside and quickly write their name down on the house they lived in so she would not forget their name. That is so great. How many times have I talked to someone only to forget their name or which house they live in? We are new to our neighborhood, so I confess that I have only visited with a few of our neighbors. People don't sit on their front porches anymore, so we don't see as many people outside when we take a walk, but I have been trying to speak to everyone on my walks. I hope to show them that I am interested in my neighbors. We can also pray for opportunities. We won't know everyone, but we can pray for opportunities to reach out to those around us.

Another thing she mentioned was that there was an older woman on her street who had no one in the area, so she planned a birthday party for her and invited all the neighbors. What an incredible idea! Thank you, Sue, for your wise insights.

One of the easiest ways to help someone in need or even just someone who just needs a bit of extra help is to take a meal. I usually take a main dish in a throw-away container so they do not have to worry about getting the container back to me. I put a salad in a large plastic bag or give a jar of applesauce, a loaf of bread or rolls, and a dessert of some sort. If there are children, I'll send cookies, but I usually do my cobbler. I am sure you have great ideas, too. Sometimes I do three meals at once and deliver them in the same day. It is easier than doing them a week apart.

One of the best things I've done is to train my children to be hospitable, caring, empathetic people. In our last neighborhood, my kids and I would take a loaf of banana or pumpkin bread to everyone when they moved in. I am sure there were some we missed, but we tried. We also made cookie plates for households on our street at Christmas time. I think it is part of our responsibility to show our children ways they can reach out and show hospitality too. A friend's family has made candy cane bread braids every Christmas for over thirty years. It is a huge undertaking. The recipe is found later in this book. Not only is this a fun thing to do, but people now look forward to receiving them each year.

Sometimes, the most helpful thing is to go visit with someone. Just to sit and listen to their stories or share life with them. People enjoy having someone come by to see them, or maybe do a small chore for them. They may not feel like they can ask you to help, but if you notice while you are visiting, then you can casually help them out. If you notice something bigger that needs doing, you can plan to come back to take care of what is needed.

Start today—right now, even. Create a family tradition to make something for someone or do a random act of kindness for someone you know who needs to know they matter to someone and that God hasn't "forgotten" them. God's gifts are meant to be shared whether you have a large home or a small one and whether you feel outgoing or not. Everyone lives in different places and has different circumstances in their lives. You know people I will never meet: hurting people who can be reached by God only through your willingness to minister (to serve) God's love to them. Your way of showing hospitality will be different than mine. Hospitality shows others how much you care about them. It shows them that you want to give them your time to prepare a place for them to feel at home—a place where they can be themselves. It doesn't matter if things are perfect, just that they feel welcome and cared for. I would encourage you to expand your ideas and look at hospitality in a new, fresh way.

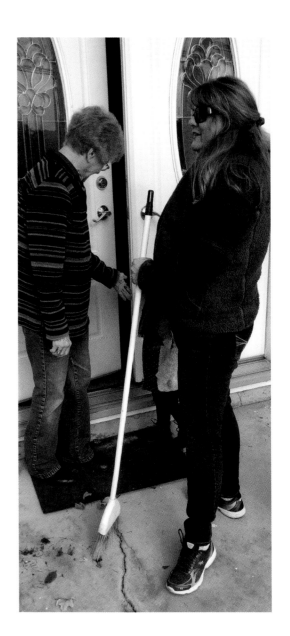

CHAPTER 2

My Story

*"By wisdom a house is built, and by understanding
it is established; and by knowledge the rooms
are filled with all precious and pleasant riches."*
—Proverbs 24:3–4

My early years were spent growing up on a horse ranch in Western Washington. My momma—we called her "Moma"—used to joke our home was just a converted chicken coop. Whether that was factually true or not, I can't say, but I do know Moma always said so. She had always been a city girl before marrying my dad, and it's likely our somewhat primitive homestead was not her favorite. It was long, with no windows on the north side, and the rustic agrarian look was not her idea of how a house should look. Moma embraced it enough to live in and rear  her children in it, but she would not allow us to have friends over. If friends did invite themselves over, she made them sit on a hard rock seat connected to the fireplace, thus giving them an incentive not to make an evening of it.

Later, in the last thirty years of her life, God transformed Moma, and she had people visit quite often; they would sit in front of her rocker and share their burdens, and she would pray and minister to them. Moma's heart of hospitality applied to family, too. Our grandparents lived next door to us on the farm. After my Grandma died, Moma would have Grandpa come to dinner at our house, and Moma was always faithful in her care of him.

Holidays can be very lonely times for shut-ins or those "parked" in nursing homes by their families who are "too busy to visit right now." Moma would always invite someone from one of the local nursing homes to come to Thanksgiving dinner.

At the time, it felt a bit awkward to me as a teen, having a stranger join us, but I have learned that we should not let that stop us from reaching out. It reminds me of where Hebrews 13:2 says, "Do not neglect to show hospitality to strangers; for by this some have entertained angels without knowing it." Maybe an angel was eating the drumstick—I'll never know until I get to Heaven.

When I got married, I was very excited to have a home to invite others to enjoy. We were married when my husband was still in college. Our small duplex was so tiny it had no eating area, and for a long time, we had no sofa or chair to sit on. So, when we invited five other couples over for dinner, I had to get "crafty" and solve my entertaining problem. I had a couple of folding tables and folding chairs so I would set up tables. There wasn't much room, but I was very happy to be able to do that and thoroughly delighted when a good time was had by all—it was the fellowship, not the floor plan, people remembered. It was March, so in the St. Patrick's Day holiday mindset, I made corned beef. I was surprised that about half my guests had never had it. It was such a fun evening, even though it was so cramped. I had a tablecloth I had gotten for our wedding and two candlesticks. We were so young, and I was so thrilled to have friends over and delighted what a success our evening was.

Soon after Craig graduated, we moved into a 750-square-foot triplex. Woohoo! I was moving up! By then, I was very much into decorating. Art is my thing, and color is very important to me. I made many things for that little home that we lived in for those five years. Our place also had a little backyard and garage! With such an abundance of space, we entertained even more, often having friends over at least a couple times a week. We had a hide-a-bed so that people could come from out of town and stay with us in that little place. Three kids later, we decided a move was in order. We needed more space, Craig had a job transfer, and we found ourselves in Boise, Idaho.

We looked at about twenty-five homes in Boise over three days. One of the last homes we saw felt best for us. The price was right, it had a great floor plan, and it was brand new! I had not grown up with a nice home—certainly not new. I somehow felt it was wrong. I now know that is not true, but at the time, I was not sure about it. We were out to breakfast with our pastor, who I knew from growing up in Washington, and he was encouraging when he said, "Some people use their homes for others. It's been given to you. I know you will use it." God speaks in different ways; we certainly felt peace about buying that house after that word from our pastor. If we hadn't, we certainly would have missed out on all the fun we had decorating that lovely home inside and out, including many happy hours spent learning more about landscaping. Having grown up in Washington State where everything just grows and there is vegetation everywhere, I had no clue that a green thumb in Idaho was a lot more complicated than in Washington, and had to learn the hard way about soil amendments and planting everything in the yard. Here in Idaho, we have hard-as-a-rock clay soil. I had never encountered this before. Why could I not put my shovel into the dirt? The first day at it, I only got about three feet dug up. A neighbor came over and explained. He said I would need a tiller and all sorts of bags of soil amendment. I wanted to have people over, so we worked hard. We were overrun with morning glory and thistles, but we tried to keep a handle on it.

My new friend Ann came by with her tiller and showed me how to till my flower beds. She was a selfless person who befriended me early on. She watched my newborn son for me and worked on art projects with me. It was wonderful to have a young woman connect with me in that first year when I did not know many people.

Another child and a dog added to our family, and we wanted more space to run around, so after six years, we looked again to move closer to Craig's work. We began looking for land to build on with bigger lots. We found a lot a mile from Craig's work. Since it was a new subdivision and they were anxious to have someone finally live there, we got a deal on it and on building the house. We remained there for eighteen years. I mention those little family details, as it's important to remember that family life goes on as you are decorating, working, landscaping, and everything else that's so essential to "living" these days. Hospitality is a mindset—a "heart-set," really—and it should be an all the time thing. Saying hello, holding the door for someone loaded down, petting a dog, offering a smile or compliment when the occasion permits—all are ways of ministering hospitality and cost us nothing!

This latest new home was my dream home, and it soon became a hub of activity. We had more space, so we had more variety in how we could be hospitable. Our new basement allowed us to host missionaries, kids from singing groups, and anyone in need of a place to land for a couple weeks. We could take people in, and by allowing them to stay with us, we shared our heart of hospitality with them.

One of the sweetest times was when my youngest daughter, Brianna Mae, asked if her friend Adrian could stay with us during spring break from college. She came

and she stayed, and she became "our Adrian." She fit right in and became like another daughter. She is still dear to my heart. Who would've dreamed that one spring break hospitable act would end up blessing us for a lifetime? God certainly does work in mysterious ways.

Ever travelled much? Ever worried about where you could do laundry? Our new home allowed us to extend hospitality with our washer and dryer. When travelers came through, I always wanted to let them know they could come and go as they pleased. I encouraged them to use our laundry room if need be and to make themselves at home.

After five years in this home, Craig said to me, "Let's build a pool." Yes! I was totally stoked. I quickly did the research on best deals and asked others who had pools what the best thing they did was and what they wished they had done. The answers were consistent, so I felt we got the best deal we could. Then I thought, *How can I use this special addition to our home?* The Lord dropped an idea into my head that children who had never learned to swim would likely jump at the chance, so our "Little Swimmers" was born, and for ten years, we opened our backyard up every Thursday, during the summers, to people of all ages. Part of the inspiration was that I knew several kids who were afraid of swimming, and I thought this might help. The amazing thing was that within a couple of weeks, those kids were soon jumping off the diving board. What's more, children who were afraid of animals were soon hugging my dog. By the last couple years, we were averaging about thirty-five people per week, sometimes up to sixty. I actually had to hire a lifeguard or stay out by the pool all afternoon just to make sure everyone was safe in the water. When we would break for lunch, I would close the pool cover. Safety came first. We had a snow cone machine, and my son, Nathan, would make snow cones for the kids. I always appreciated teens coming to help. It was a tiring day, but so worth it. Sometimes hospitality is shaved ice on a hot summer day.

We enjoyed hosting our annual church picnic and usually had about 150 people to dinner and pool party each summer. This took help from many people. I am not great with details. I come up with the idea, and I am not a perfectionist, so I need people in my life to make things happen. But guess what? There are people who have a heart to help and are delighted to assist in making parties happen. I could never have done any of these many things without all my dear friends who helped. Every year, my close friend, Marsha, would come help weed my acre and a half before the church picnic. Many times, her husband also came. They are amazing friends. It wasn't unusual for me, in the middle of a big happening at our house, to walk a person down my driveway and visit or be off to the side, talking or praying one on one with someone. Yet the helpers were keeping the hospitality organized, and when I would walk into my kitchen, the "doers" would be refilling trays and cleaning. I understand what Jesus meant about Mary, but nothing would get done without the Marthas. I seriously believe that. I am more of a Mary than a Martha most of the time, but I am so very thankful for the Marthas in my life. I really think we need to be a combo of both. We first need to listen to Jesus like Mary and be a doer like Martha. For without really listening to Him, what good is serving?

"Now as they were traveling along, He entered a certain village; and a woman named Martha welcomed Him into her home. And she had a sister named Mary, who moreover was listening to the Lord's word, seated at His feet. But Martha was distracted with all her preparations; and she came up to Him, and said, 'Lord, do you not care that my sister has left me to do all the serving alone? Then tell her to help me.' But the Lord answered and said to her, 'Martha, Martha, you are worried and bothered about so many things; but only a few things are necessary, really only one, for Mary has chosen the good part, which shall not be taken away from her.'" (Luke 10:38–42)

One of the most fun things for outside parties was my cooler. I had a cooler on a stand. I always had a sign on it saying, "Aunt Nicki's Cooler." I had small sodas, juice and water bottles on ice. The kids all knew that they could each take a special drink from "Aunt Nicki's Cooler." It warmed my heart when they'd run up to me and politely ask if they could have a drink. Those kids have grown bigger now but they will always be dear to my heart. We had inside events there too and even built on an addition room to be able to have a larger room for people to hang out. It was 28 by 28 feet with shelves on one side, a fireplace on one end and surrounded by windows and French doors to the pool. It was a great place to host events. I admit I loved sharing my yard the most because I love being outside.

Sometimes we can do simple things for others. When our son, Nathan, was in high school he wanted to invite a few friends over to swim on the last day of school. A small group of about five of his friends came over. I quickly started grabbing things

from my pantry. I dumped crackers into bowls, made popcorn, and found some random cans of soda. I will never forget that one of the neighbor boys came inside, saw these few snacks, and said, "You did all this for us?" Wow. It was such an easy thing to do, but it's also so easy to just say you don't want to deal with it. I'm so glad I just said yes. Little things make all the difference!

There are seasons to life, and becoming empty nesters brought changes to our home. Three years ago, we decided to downsize since the kids were all grown and we wanted to have a smaller yard. I did not embrace the idea at first, but I was ready for the next adventure. For the past three years, we have lived in the historical district in a home that was built in 1907. Being people who don't generally hire out work, we began the task of painting all the interior and redoing several rooms. When we decided to remodel our master bath, it was quite the project. I am so proud of my husband, Craig, and all his hard work. He did almost all the work to renovate the bathroom from electrical to sheet rock to plumbing and paint. My son-in-law, Shane, helped with demo and sheetrock. Nathan helped with maneuvering the tub and vanity through the doors. The remodel took about four months. Craig had gotten deals on several things online, so we had a vanity, a bathtub, plumbing fixtures, and lighting all in boxes in our living room. We host a small group Bible study at our home each week, and we knew we would not cancel because of this enormous pile of construction supplies, equipment, debris, and dust. No one cared. We enjoy our time together too much to let that bother any of us. Hospitality makes the difference—nobody complains when they're having fun and being blessed.

However, to be completely honest, it is true that a couple hours before Bible study, I usually run around and touch up the house, get out dishes for dinner, figure out beverages, and get things set up. Our dog, Ginger, knows the drill. She knows people are coming over, and she waits by the door because mommy is acting like people are coming. One time my friend, Lyn, came about thirty minutes early. She asked what she could do to help, and I said I was doing OK, but I was sweaty and running around. Then she said in her witty way, trying to calm me down and help me regain my perspective, "You know, I have a friend writing a book called *It's Not About the Pie*." She loved me enough to get my attention with that bit of humorous sarcasm, and I got the message. Here I was stressing while writing a book that tells others not to stress. I do race around when people come, and have even been known to paint a mural before a gathering—yes, it's true. I think it's that "art thing." I have painted a scene on a wall as part of my decorating, sometimes hours before people have come over. I think we all want to be prepared when people are coming over. There is nothing wrong with that; it is a good thing. However, we must think about the purpose of hospitality, which is not perfection.

My college friend, Re, had this to say about her house and "perfection":

> I have piles of stuff: piles of papers, magazines, laundry, dishes, mail, newspapers, random boxes. With three children, I had piles of backpacks, toys, and school papers. You may have some of the same piles as I do, or they may vary. That's OK. Don't let the stacks of stuff in your house keep you from inviting people in. I used to always apologize for the messiness

of my house to my friend Joanne and give an excuse. "I'm sorry about the mess, but the kids were sick. Forgive the piles of mail, I have had a hectic week." And so on. Then I realized that I said that every time she came over. The messiness wasn't an anomaly; it was really the norm! But she didn't care. It didn't matter because a perfectly tidy home was not necessary to be welcoming.

We didn't always have a nice house or the most organized or neat home, but I still needed to welcome people. Why else had I been given my home? I think most of us, no matter what stage in life, can be thankful for our home and can use it to help someone and we do not need to apologize for it. The beauty of it all is that God can use imperfect people to perfectly bless other imperfect people with everyone having a good time in the process!

CHAPTER 3

Aunt Betty

"Be hospitable to one another without complaint, as each one has received a special gift, employ it in serving one another, as good stewards of the manifold grace of God."
—1 Peter 4:9–10

After Craig graduated from Cal Poly, we moved up the coast to San Jose, where all good software engineers go. We were sad as we drove up the 101 leaving all our dear friends behind. I was about five months pregnant when Craig started work, leaving me to set up the apartment and find my way around Silicon Valley. We only had one car at the time, and if I wanted to go anywhere, I needed to take him to work each morning. We had no idea that the San Jose area was six cities all blended together. We got our first apartment in Cupertino, which was much higher in price. We did this because the HP site Craig was to work at was in Cupertino. Then, after only a month or two, we realized we could move a few miles away and pay a fraction of what that apartment cost. After only about six months and the birth of our daughter, we moved to San Jose. It wasn't any farther for Craig to go to work, either. Our new triplex was smaller than the apartment in Cupertino, but it was more like having a house (with a garage and a little yard), and it was over twice the size of our first home.

One of the very best things about moving up the coast to the San Jose area was meeting Aunt Betty and Uncle Bill. They are not blood relations, but they became family. You may have those people in your life who are closer to you than family and become embedded into your heart. They were parents of friends of ours from where we had just moved. I think the very first week (or if not, the second week) after we moved, I got a call from Betty. She had a thick New York accent. She asked if she could drive me around to some fabric or craft stores and show me where they were. I knew no one in the area so I said, "sure." And so it began.

This petite Italian woman became so instrumental in my life. We became close friends, not just because she took me places but for what she input into our lives.

She would bring us meals, and she came and walked my babies in the evenings those first couple weeks after they were born. She did my ironing and prayed for us. Her husband, Bill, was into model trains and would take Craig to train shows. We were invited over for Thanksgiving one year, first time I ever had manicotti with turkey. It's great!

When Nathan was born a few days before Christmas, we brought him home from the hospital on Christmas Eve. New baby, biggest holiday of the year, and oh yeah, did I mention Craig's folks were coming to visit for Christmas and to see the new baby in two days on the 26th? Well, I did mention it to Aunt Betty as I was on the phone talking to her trying to figure out easy meals to make for when they came. She suggested lasagna. I thought she was crazy since I hardly ever made it due to it being so time consuming. I told her that and said I hated having to boil the noodles. She replied that you weren't supposed to boil the noodles. What? How is that possible? Then she told me how she made her lasagna. I was highly skeptical. But it turned out perfect and I have never again boiled the noodles. Although we no longer live near this dear couple, they will always remain close to me. I have kept the baby quilts she made and many memories of those times. And guess who I think of every time I have lasagna?

Here was a woman who, without ever having met me, reached out to encourage a younger woman. This is an incredible example of someone giving their time, and energy to help someone else. I can

only hope that someday I can be as helpful to someone else. I think we can pray for God to bring people into our lives for us to help. Yes, she blessed me that week—but her love has inspired and challenged me to copy her example for a lifetime (I've also shared her lasagna recipe, too).

Sometimes chances to be hospitable may be completely random, totally spontaneous surprises, and maybe you will only have one chance to talk to that person. I was driving down the freeway one day and saw a young woman running across five lanes to the side of the road. I saw a car on the other side, across the median. She was carrying a small gas can. I decided it was a fairly safe scenario, so I pulled over, rolled down my window, and asked her if she needed a ride. She got in, looked at me, and said, "Worst … day … ever." Tears then came. She said her wallet had gotten stolen and she was trying to get to someone's house to get money to buy gas to get to work. I then asked how she would buy the gas. She opened her fist, and in it was about fifty pennies from her car. Her fist was red from being clenched tightly while she ran across the freeway. I took her to the gas station, bought her gas, and drove her back to her car. She asked where I was headed and if I'd be late. I told her about my first book, *Not Really a Princess*, and what it was about. She wrote down the title and my name. I have prayed for her over the past couple years. We don't always know why people come into our lives. We need to be kind to everyone we meet. We don't know their story, and we don't need to. We need to be available to help and willing to listen.

It doesn't matter how big or how small of a thing you do, just do it. Be an Aunt Betty.

CHAPTER 4

Take Them in and Be a Blessing

*"True hospitality consists of giving the best
of yourself to your guests."*
—Eleanor Roosevelt

I have already told you about our Adrian that we took in over spring break. Well, she ended up staying with us for a few months. She made herself right at home. We loved her like a daughter. She even played on our softball team that summer. I would never trade that time. Providing lodging for someone is a great thing. She blessed us more than we blessed her. Am I hesitant when those opportunities arise? Absolutely. But I do not feel it should hinder me. And for those that believe I must just be an outgoing person, it is not always true. Sometimes I am way out of my comfort zone. Never forget that the person you are helping might be terrified of you, too.

Have you taken any of those personality tests? I had to take them in college and since then on several occasions had to take them for a class I was in or maybe at a retreat. My results have been very consistent over the past 30 years. I am right on the line, part extrovert and part introvert. Sometimes my fears take over and I cannot talk to someone I do not know, other times it comes with ease. The more prayed-up I am, the easier I find it to respond when that little inner voice says, "Act."

I recently had close friends, Harold and Elisa, spend the weekend at our home. Their son was going to college at the university near us and it was move-in weekend. They needed to come and we were camping, but they stayed at our house and when we returned Sunday night, we were able to go to dinner with them and stay up visiting. The following week I would be staying at their house on my way to some author events in California. Driving home from our dinner, she told me that she will never forget the first week she was at our church 25 years before. We had invited them to lunch after church, and was I very humbled and amazed when she told me that lunch invitation was the whole reason they had stayed at our church. Wow. And it had so nearly not happened as I had been very hesitant to ask out people I did not know. But my mentor and dear friend, Ruthanne, came up to me that very Sunday and said, "Nicki, there is a new family here and you need to invite them to lunch." Sigh. Ok, I am instructed to do this, I need to do this. And I am so glad I did. What if I hadn't responded and been hospitable? We would have all missed out on decades of fellowship and dear friendship.

That's not the end of the story, as the following week when I was at their house, Elisa told me that twenty-five years ago, when she had been to my house, I had projects going everywhere and kids working on crafts. The house was not perfect, and I was working on making wreaths for an upcoming craft show. My dining room table has always been a workspace for me, so it usually has working materials on it. We visited as I was putting my wreath together and then I handed her the wreath. I have no recollection of this at all. She said she has kept this wreath on her door for twenty-five years at Christmas time. She said she was a young mom and I had an impact on her. You just never know. She has had a book club reading my first book and doing the study questions. She has told the women, "This is the woman who made my wreath!" We have an impact on so many in our lives and we have no clue. You will have no idea your eternal impact or how far the ripples of your hospitality extend on the seas of life until you get to Heaven. Our lives, examples, and kindnesses really can make an eternal difference.

We have friends who work for a mission agency and travel much of time. They came and stayed in our basement and it was the week before our annual church picnic. I was outside in 95-degree weather planting flowers near the pool. My friend,

Pam felt totally at home and got down on her knees to get dirty and sweat with me doing my plantings. She blessed me. This kind act became a very tangible blessing to us as she planted with me. That was such a wonderful gift. Helping each other is so important. We have had many missionaries stay with us over the years. My goal is to always make them feel at home. They can just rest and not feel like they are in the spotlight or be in "ministry mode."

I can remember being in a music group from my college and staying at a different home each night when on tour. I remember being in Northern California and four of us going home with a family after our concert. The mom led us to a huge family room with a big rock fireplace and two hide-a-beds. She had made treats and put them in the room. She then turned around and told us we could watch a movie and to have a fun evening. She then shut two huge pocket doors. A free night! We could just feel at home and not have to sit and visit with our hosts all night. I have tried to do this when we have kids over from travelling groups. Use the hot tub, pool, washer, TV. Relax. What a blessing, just being allowed to "be."

I also have taken great thought in what food to make for at home guests as well as meals to take to people. Having travelled with a group, I know it's not great to have spaghetti five nights in a row. I try to do something out of the ordinary. Think VARIETY. Something that I think they may not get very often on their journey. And you know, you don't have to take a meal to someone just because they have had a baby or because they are ill. You can make four loaves of banana bread and deliver it to four people just because it'd be fun for them to receive something special and unexpected.

Sometimes we may feel prompted to invite someone over but maybe fear stops you. Cross out the word "fear"—write in "Devil." Do you really think the Devil wants you to minister, relieve stress, feed, entertain, pray with, inspire? You are his biggest headache when you share God's love. Ignore the fear! Do what you feel God is directing you to do.

I am so happy that I invited my friend Jenn to our home for Christmas one year. I was a merchandiser at a large department store for many years. I made several close friends there that are still my friends. One of my friends was a quiet young woman from Washington. She was a university student and usually rode her bike to work at 4:30 in the morning. She was a hard worker and had a lovely smile. I discovered that she usually did not go home for holidays, so I invited her over. She came several times, and I appreciated her coming. She moved away a few years ago, and I miss that time with her. For many Christmases, she would sit and knit, knit, knit for hours on end. I think it was a stress reliever for her with the hustle and bustle of the holiday work routine. She was very talented and would knit sweaters and socks! How very easy it is to invite someone over for a holiday. Not only does it give them a place to be on the holiday but it blesses you as well. It is a blessing being a blessing; when we open our doors, it allows God a chance to sneak a blessing in!

For years, a friend had a gathering at her house every Sunday night, which they called "Life Group." Some years they had up to thirty people, with half of them children under the age of twelve. Some years there were only about a dozen people, with five of those being her own family. Their home is not very large. People were in the living room, the dining area, and outside. She said, "Our carpet is old, our couch is old, and our outdoor chairs were the old chairs from the church fellowship hall that had holes in the vinyl. Sometimes things spilled, or broke. But that was OK. Old carpet—another spill is no big deal. I am not the best housekeeper. Things get very messy and cluttered at my house—especially when my kids were young. Opening our home every Sunday was a great catalyst for me to tidy up once a week." Even though things were not perfect, she came to see that she did not need to get stressed out about people coming over. Everyone enjoyed each other's company. They were able to talk and really get to know each other. It was always a potluck, and each person or family brought some food to share. Sometimes there were an abundance of leftovers; other times, almost every scrap was eaten, but no one went hungry. The point of their Life Group was to share life with each other, not showcase a home or gorge themselves on a banquet.

Welcoming people in regardless of our messy house, no food prepared, the time sacrifice, all shows your commitment to following God's leading. You may need to douse your fears and follow your heart. God will direct you if you ask for His help.

I want people to feel like they can sit on our sofa and put their feet up, that they can grab something from the cupboard, a book from the shelf and take a nap in front of the fire. I want them to feel like they are family and not an outsider. And I am always amazed that I feel so extremely blessed by them having come into our home.

CHAPTER 5

Unexpected Need—Unexpected Help

"Contributing to the needs of the saints, practicing hospitality."
—Romans 12:13

We all have friends, family and church members who come across severe health issues or financial problems. We all go through rough times. Tough times are real opportunities to help God answer heartfelt prayers prayed in desperate hours when someone sees no way out unless God intervenes. Tell you a secret: God often answers prayers through His people getting involved in tangible ways with food, shelter, money, a ride to the doctor, or … (fill in the blank—you've needed help before).

Over twenty-six years ago, my oldest daughter was diagnosed with diabetes. She was only six years old. I spent the first day reading everything I could, learning, and crying. I had several friends who helped out with my three younger kids. My friend, Julie, was a homeschool mom. She did not hesitate to take the kids that first morning so I could go to school and talk with the school nurse, office staff, and teacher. Then, in the afternoon, she delivered them to my friend. Susan later told me that Julie had said to her, "It just needed to happen." She was impressed by the sacrifice of time Julie had made when it was not convenient. Thank you, Jesus. Julie ministered that day in such a simple way that made a big difference for me on one of the worst days of my life while I was overwhelmed with worry for my daughter.

Here is a story my friend Ruthanne shared with me about a time when her family was blessed by someone going above the expected normal behavior at just the right time to abundantly share with her family. Remember, this is a true story:

> Thanksgiving Eve. Our bags are packed, ready for the trip from Boise to Eastern Washington to join the rest of our family at my brother's home for the holiday. Around midnight the phone rings. My younger sister says, "Pray. Dad's had a

heart attack." We pray—surely he can't die. He's a pastor, and only 61. Mom and his church need him.

But a few minutes later, "He's gone. The EMTs couldn't save him. How soon can you get here?"

We quickly add funeral clothes to our luggage, wake up the kids, and head over the mountains toward Seattle.

My brothers' families arrive before us, and we all sit around Mom's kitchen in the parsonage, ask questions, cry a little, hug each other, and try to think straight.

Suddenly, the door opens and in walks one of Dad's young deacons, followed by his wife and kids. Each one carries a platter of food—their complete Thanksgiving dinner. They arrange it on Mom's table, hug us all, and leave. I'll never forget their generous, kind act of understanding.

Hebrews 13:16 encourages us when it states, "And do not neglect doing good and sharing; for with such sacrifices God is pleased." I just saw an old memo I wrote in my Bible that says, "life goal." I am not exactly sure when I wrote that but I am continuing to work toward that goal.

Wow, talk about an act of compassion and generosity! And what an example for their children!

There is a young mom and dad at our church who had a very traumatic time when their oldest child was young. He was in and out of the hospital so much and my heart broke for them. I asked Jennifer to share her and Kevin's story:

My son was diagnosed unexpectedly at three months old with hydrocephalus. A condition where spinal fluid builds up in your head, putting pressure on your brain and you need a shunt placed to correct it. It was a busy and stressful day that eventually ended with my newborn baby having brain surgery. Our pediatrician first gave us the diagnosis and then stepped out of the room to call a neurosurgeon. While she was out, I said to my husband, "We have to be strong for Blake and a light for God!" That night, Blake had surgery. I remember my in-laws, family friends, and our pastor and his wife coming to visit with us in the hospital. This helped distract us for a little while. After Blake's surgery, he looked amazing and we were able to go home. I had one friend come and visit with me that following week. This meant so much to me because I truly didn't know this person all that well at the time. She just sat and listened to me about what Blake had, how the surgery went, how he's recovering. I wasn't alone through this! Time went on—eighteen months, to be exact—and Blake became sick on and off due to his shunt malfunctioning inside his head. This process to make him feel better took three years and two more brain surgeries. Also, I should mention that in those three years, I had two more babies. I needed help. We made it through with help from our parents and our church family. So much prayer, the offering of meals, hugs, babysitting for our other children, and a huge but simple blessing was cards in the mail. Our mailbox was full of medical insurance info and hospital bills, and it was nice to receive a happy card in the middle of all of it. Blake is now a thriving, healthy, and smart five-year-old.

So many people gave of their time and sent many prayers upward. And one of the special things she remembers is people sending a simple card. Taking five minutes to jot a note or send a pretty or funny card can mean so much to someone going through a difficult time. Everyone has five minutes—use it to reach out to someone.

Here's another instance of hospitality making the difference: Our church has a family whose dad has had serious medical issues for a very long time. John shares his story of how the church helped them through this difficult time that is still ongoing:

> Life was moving along well for me in 2017. I had been retired for about two years, golfing, pursuing photography, gardening, and helping with the cooking and cleaning, as my wife, Candy, was not yet retired. The Lord was using me as well. I was a deacon in our church, taught Sunday school, and Candy and I held a home study group in our home. Life seemed to be pretty good right then, but that was about to come crashing down.
>
> In May of 2017, I ended up in the hospital in septic shock, which led to a gallbladder removal, and then to liver disease. I spent about four months in and out of the hospital here in Boise, Idaho, with the next nine months in Phoenix, Arizona, for treatment at the Mayo Clinic, with cirrhosis of the liver.

I ended up having two liver transplants within two weeks of each other. This happened because the first transplant failed, due to a blood clot and it needed to be replaced.

During this time of illness, transplants, and numerous infections, I almost died three times. In my entire life, I cannot remember a time that I have been that ill as well as asking, "Why me, God? Why me?" This was not my first major illness. In 2010, I fought cancer for eight to nine months only to once again be fighting for my life. I was asking God, "Why something like this again?"

Through this searching and questioning I never lost my faith, or trust in God. I just did not understand why, or for that matter, "Why me?" One night as I talked and prayed to God, seeking solace and answers from Him, I asked Him why this was happening to me. "Why, Father, would You bring me this far only to take my life?" I remember, it was around two or three in the morning, I was wiped out. Lying there, totally beaten down, I told God, "Fine this is how You want things, I submit to Your will. I do not like it, I do not agree with it, but You are God, my God and I submit." Then miraculously I fell asleep, where sleep had been eluding me before.

The next morning, I woke up completely at peace with my situation. I was still not sure if I would live or die, but I was at peace. God intervened—He answered my crying out to Him. God was showing me that it was not about me, it's about Him and bringing Him glory and honor through my situation. It was about seeking Him through prayer and asking Him, "What is it You have called me to do for You? How can I, through this darkness show Your light and bring You glory?" That meant whether I lived, or God called me home, I lived for Him.

It was also during this time that God let me know I was not alone in this. For so long I was focused on myself, my hurts, my pain, my suffering, that I had forgotten how many people I had praying for me and helping us out. God stepped in, He put me on the hearts of my friends and family.

There are times when people will tell friends or other people "I'll pray for you," in times of trouble, sickness, or distress. I do it and I pray, but this went way beyond anything I had ever experienced or imagined. The amount of love, compassion, and friendship layered on Candy and me was simply amazing.

From the time when we reached the Mayo Clinic in Phoenix, Candy and I realized that we were going to struggle financially. Struggle is an understatement. We had two households that we were financially responsible for, food, gas for the car, as well as various sundry things we would need while living in Phoenix. Both Candy and I wondered if we might need to declare bankruptcy. It never happened. We never missed a house, or rent payment. We always had groceries as needed and were able to put gas in the car. Why? Because God put on the hearts of our church family to step in and see that we were not in want. We were in Phoenix for eight to nine months and never had a financial problem. Our immediate family, friends, and especially our church family loved on us in ways that are simply hard to explain, except for God.

These folks also sent around one to two hundred cards, text messages, and emails to us. A member of our church flew (in his own plane) our senior pastor to Phoenix just to see us. Do you realize how encouraging that is, to get a card, text, or email, while lying in a hospital bed, or confined to a chair in an apartment. Those things lit up my day and were a great source of encouragement.

Currently I am still recovering my strength and health. God intervened in my life. He has been my guide through this time of darkness and has moved me into His light. He used his people to encourage and help me throughout this time. Their kindness and generosity were part of God's care for me. Why did He not take me home when it looked as though He would? My only answer is "I'm not done with you yet. I have a plan for you My child."

It's difficult to read that without tearing up.

2 Corinthians chapter 8 has the chapter heading "great generosity" in my Bible. It is a great lesson in how the body of Christ works. Sometimes a church will sacrifice to help its members. This blesses not only the recipient but also the giver. I love verses 7–8:

"But just as you abound in everything, in faith and utterance and knowledge and in all earnestness, and in the love we inspired in you, see that you abound in this gracious work also. I am not speaking this as a command, but as proving through the earnestness of others the sincerity of your love also."

I know in my heart that I am sometimes prompted to help someone after visiting with them, but my week continues and I forget about it. Ah, dear reader, if we can only remember to act on those ways to help. We can take meals, and assist in whatever way we can, but sometimes it is a bigger issue that takes months or maybe years to resolve. This can be very wearying for caregivers or those with the long-term illness. So I have to ask, "What would be helpful for me to do?"

A new friend of mine, Coral was recently sharing her story with me, and I thought it was a wonderful example of how the church had filled in the blanks and provided needs when they were blindsided by her young son's (age four at the time) cancer diagnosis.

> In April of 2016, our son was diagnosed with cancer. Pre–B Cell ALL, to be exact. If you can imagine someone sucking all the air out of your lungs in under a second, that's close to what the diagnosis felt like.
>
> As our world flipped upside down and twisted inside out, the Lord pulsed through the Body, causing them to come alive in new and meaningful ways. Our boy's story touched their hearts and they in turn touched our lives. A group held a prayer vigil at a local church. Another group coordinated a Chick-fil-A fundraiser (where we became the highest-grossing event at that location). A few brought meals. Many gave money. Out-of-towners purchased love gifts from our boys' Wish Lists which kept their spirits up. A select few were allowed to visit us in the hospital, where we lived for almost a month. We received so many gift cards for gas and groceries. It was a strange season

that embodied the Christmas spirit while spanning months of time in the wrong part of the year.

The most meaningful blessing was *money*. I know that sounds materialistic, but money was the one resource we didn't have enough of and needed the most (we became a single income household because I had to quit my job to care for our son). A cancer journey is one of the most expensive journeys a person or family could ever face—despite most of the treatment being covered by insurance. Beyond the cost of conventional treatment was the exponentially increasing cost of the alternative modalities we needed to employ for our son's thrivorship. A normal diet wasn't going to help him thrive, he needed higher quality food and added nutritionals. Essential oils became a staple in our daily routine. A therapy trike was necessary to help him reclaim his muscles and physical abilities. New cookware was needed because we learned ours was toxic. Acupuncture, not covered by insurance, was another modality we employed to help his little body cope with the trauma of cancer treatment. And there was more.

So many blessings were bestowed upon our family and there was no denying the presence and intention of the Lord. He supplied our needs and sustained us in ways I still can't quantify. I was also very specific in sharing our needs so that no one's resources were wasted because, in a situation like ours, it is important to note that the best of intentions can be lost on the recipient when their need is so great and the gifts are not appropriate. The Lord continues to supply our needs despite the majority of our support having vanished long before our son's treatment ended.

Years ago, our friends Neal and Patti had triplets. I had never known someone who had triplets. We had time to prepare for this and a schedule was set up for people to assist them. (This is a good way to help you to *not* forget.) I mean, if you can imagine how difficult twins are, then add one more child into the mix. They were such amazing parents. They had schedules to make sure no one missed a feeding or changing. I asked her recently about that time. Here is her story.

Though our triplets' birth brought instant joy and chaos, God used our church to keep us afloat. Preemies take twice as long to feed compared to full-term babies, and once the third child is fed, the first is ready to wake up and start the process all over again. Our pastor's wife organized feeding teams to help three nights a week—what a welcome gift!

I never heard what sort of schedule they had with three babies teething at the same time!

Patti wasn't always a mother: she was an MK (missionary's kid) growing up, and I asked her if she had any hospitality stories about how God blessed them through the intervention of strangers. Here are a few blessings she recalls:

Growing up the daughter of missionaries, I watched God use people in very creative, loving ways. Some of my favorite memories include:

- Donation of a Disneyland trip for our family
- A loan of a motorhome with "gas coupons" (turns out the coupons were $20 bills)
- A sweet man in our home church who would randomly hand us money for pizza after church
- A store owner in CA who decided to delete one Mercedes from his fleet and put the money towards missions
- The many families who fed us as we travelled the West Coast on deputation
- The Mexican nationals who made special meals for us: tamales and (my favorite) goat in mole sauce

All the love and care shown to Ruthanne, Jenn, John, Coral and Patti have not only blessed and influenced their own lives, but are wonderful examples of how we all can do things, large or small, to help in times of need. Look at the good accomplished by yielding to God's "little inner voice" saying, "Get involved. Make a difference." Not only were these families blessed, you today are encouraged, inspired, maybe even incited to deliberate acts of hospitality by reading their stories!

CHAPTER 6

God's Compassion— Giving to Strangers

"Do not neglect to show hospitality to strangers, for by this some have entertained angels without knowing it."
—Hebrews 13:2

In my first book, *Not Really a Princess*, I talk about three women overcoming adversity. It is autobiographical, my personal story of how my family and I went through some very tough times during my younger years and how strangers reached out to us with God's love and care. Not only did they share Jesus with us, but they shared their love in a tangible way. We became believers in Christ through their Christian love and "hospitality" that led us to a little Baptist church in Western Washington, and that has made all the difference in our lives. God used strangers to bless us, just as He can use you to bless others.

I was a young teen when my dad died at the age of 58. It was sudden, and he did not leave a will. We had no savings, thirty-one horses to feed, and no income. My mom, sister, and I despaired. It seemed like there was no hope for the future. What would we do? How would we live? We sold twenty-eight horses about a month later. The man cheated us out of the full amount we should have received. We could not make our tax payment on our land. The little church we began to attend was totally different from where we had attended years before and seemed more "real" to me. I had never been around such people. The love and care and sacrifice of our church family was a completely new thing to me. These people always brought their Bibles to church and were thoroughly studying it. At the time, I was only thirteen and had not attended many churches, but no matter. I had never been to a place like this before, nor had I ever believed people could care so much outside a fairy tale. My sister, Lisa, and I were invited to youth group and quickly plugged in to all the fun activities that were planned. Within four months, my mom and Lisa had both accepted Jesus Christ as their Savior and I was soon to follow. The verses our church was memorizing were Romans 12:1–2,

"Therefore I urge you, brethren, by the mercies of God, to present your bodies a living and holy sacrifice, acceptable to God, which is your spiritual service of worship. And do not be conformed to this world, but be transformed by the renewing of your mind, that you may prove what the will of God is, that which is good and acceptable and perfect."

We were so surrounded by love and "Christian hospitality" that I can't really remember what the final thing that encouraged me to accept Christ was, but I know that the Bible started making sense to me. I understood that there had been a rift between God and me. I had thought of Him as aloof and unrelatable. As I began studying the New Testament, I saw that was not the case at all, that God loved me and cared about me as an individual. In fact, God loved me so much He sent His Son to earth and to die to bridge that gap between me and God. God was holy and just and must punish sin. Jesus died for my sin and if I was the only person on earth He would have still died.

Jesus was our sacrifice. We are called to also sacrifice. And sometimes that means that what we do for others is not convenient and we may have to go out of our box a little bit … or a lot. I always try to remind myself that no matter how much I might have to go outside my box, my "inconvenience" does not begin to compare with what Jesus sacrificed to redeem me.

I want to tell you about a woman named Amy Carmichael. She was a Protestant missionary in India. She served there for 55 years without furlough and wrote many books. Amy dedicated her life to God's service and did not want anything to deter her from doing as much work for God as she could. While ministering in India, she became aware of young women being dedicated to the temple at very young ages

to live in moral and spiritual danger. She took in an eight-year-old girl whose parents had sold her to the temple to be a prostitute, but the little girl would run away again and again, escaping. They branded her hands so she would not escape again, but she did yet again, which was when Amy learned of her and took her in. Amy kept taking in other children to raise on her own. In 1927, this became the Dohnavur Fellowship. In 1931, Amy had a serious fall and became an invalid for the rest of her life. She continued to write and identified leaders to take her place and continue rescuing children for Jesus. Her life-long mission of "Christian Hospitality," officially known as the Dohnavur Fellowship, continues to this very day. What a difference love can make!

Amy Carmichael sacrificed everything for others. I realize not everyone is able to do this but I hope this book will encourage all of us to seek out opportunities to meet others' needs. This includes me. What can I do this very week? Do you know any young children who need to learn of Jesus? Could you invite them to church with your kids?

A word of warning: It is true, sometimes being hospitable is a sacrifice. You may have to drive fifteen miles to deliver that meal or visit that person in need. Maybe the person seems unappreciative. Perhaps you just do not want to go that extra mile. I totally get it. I have been there myself. I think of Mary washing Jesus' feet with expensive perfume.

"Jesus, therefore, six days before the Passover, came to Bethany where Lazarus was, whom Jesus had raised from the dead. So they made Him a supper there; and Martha was serving, but Lazarus was one of those reclining at the table with Him. Mary therefore took a pound of very costly perfume of pure nard, and anointed the feet of Jesus, and wiped His feet with her hair; and the house was filled with the fragrance of the perfume. But Judas Iscariot, one of His disciples, who was intending to betray Him, said, 'Why was this perfume not sold for 300 denarii, and given to poor people?' Now he said this not because he was concerned about the poor, but because he was a thief, and as he had the money box, he used to pilfer what was put into it. Jesus therefore said, 'Let her alone, in order that she may keep it for the day of My burial. For the poor you always have with you, but you do not always have Me.'" (John 12:1–8,)

Mary's heart was in the right place. She was seeing beyond the cost to meet a need in that moment; nobody else was worried about Jesus's dirty feet. I believe it can often be a sacrifice to give to others. Not just financially but also not always the best time. How often I have thought, well, I would love to meet that need for someone but this is not a great week for me to help. Sometimes we just need to make it happen. We might not be the one in charge, but we can be the one to start the ball rolling with an aptly timed question or an offer to help organize by being the first to volunteer to take part.

Sometimes our local church body needs to reach out. My church is a great example of a missions-minded church. It is important that we remember the needs within the body of the local church, and also those persons in need in our local communities.

Another example: We have many people close to us who have worked in various ministries. My oldest daughter, Jessica, was a grant writer for our local rescue mission. I learned a lot about this organization through her involvement. Not only is there the main ministry to house and feed homeless men, but there is also a women and children's ministry and a safe house for abused women. The rescue mission takes kids to school and provides backpacks and school supplies. These kids don't want to look like they are homeless. They want cool clothes and cute backpacks. Sometimes we give our worst items to charity. They can't use them and often recycle the clothes. How fun is it for a woman to have a killer outfit for a job interview or for a child to have school shoes that are new? This is so important, maybe read this twice: people in need have feelings, and everyone has dignity. Everyone needs to be treated like they really matter and not like "here, take this." I personally will not give anything to a charity I would not use myself or that I would be ashamed to see a family member wearing or using. I want to act like I'm giving to Jesus. If you'd be fine with Jesus wearing or eating what you gave, then you're probably OK. We have the verse that the Golden Rule is taken from in Matthew 7:12, "In everything, therefore, treat people the same way you want them to treat you, for this is the Law and Prophets."

I used to be a merchandiser at a large department store. One year, when the winter coats went to $9.99, I was able to purchase thirty coats with my store discount. I felt bad that they all looked the same, but I knew they were warm. I was not able to deliver them, so a friend took them down to the mission. She said that she heard women ask, "Are those for *us*?" They were so happy to have a *new* coat. Wow. Then it hit me that I had often given things that were not even wearable.

Let's look at what Jesus said concerning hospitality to strangers and how big a deal it is to Him:

"And all the nations will be gathered before Him, and He will separate them from one another, as the shepherd separates the sheep from the goats and He will put the sheep on His right and the goats on the left. Then the King will say to those on His right, 'Come you who are blessed of My Father, inherit the kingdom prepared for you from the foundation of the world. For I was hungry and you gave Me something to eat; I was thirsty and you gave Me drink; I was a stranger and you invited Me in; naked and you clothed Me. I was sick and you visited Me; I was in prison and you came to Me.' Then the righteous will answer Him, saying, 'Lord, when did we see You hungry, and feed You, or thirsty and give You drink? And when did we see You a stranger, and invite You in, or naked and clothe You? And when did we see you sick, or in prison and come to You?' And the King will answer and say to them, 'Truly, I say to you, to the extent that you did it to one of these brothers of Mine, even the least of them, you did it to Me.'" (Matthew 25:32–40)

We are not to ignore the plight of those who suffer from hunger, homelessness, or sickness. Jesus does not say how we are to meet this need. It may mean to give them resources to learn how to grow food or build homes. But we can use our own resources to help. I hope we do not take what we have for granted. I am sure that I am not always counting my blessings, but I hope that I continue to be thankful, no matter what my circumstances are. I do not think we can really help others fully unless we appreciate what we have ourselves. Realize the blessings you have, and use them to give to strangers as well as to those who are close to you.

PART 2

Favorite Recipes

"There is no love sincerer than the love of food."
—George Bernard Shaw

For years, I have been using some of my favorite recipes from my family as I am sure you do too! Let's face it, there is no really "new" recipe; everyone makes the recipes handed down to them their own, by adding or subtracting or combining new ingredients together. That's half the fun of cooking: making smiles! Having said that, I am going to share with you (so you can "steal" them) a few recipes I have gleaned from friends or family or just devised on my own at a time of entertaining emergency. Try to become a "scratch cook." Let me explain: My mother-in-law recently passed away; the last time I saw her, we were talking about food, and she made a comment to me: "Well, you are a scratch cook, so you can do that." I had never heard that term before, but I understood her meaning. I rarely use a recipe when I cook. I follow recipes more with baked things because I want it to rise, but all in all, I seldom do. So then why do I have a recipe section in this book? Because we have many people over, and I have had so many compliments on some recipes that I decided to share them with you.

I will tell you that I do add a little of this and a little of that but have tried my best to make the recipes concise for you. Some of these recipes are very special to me and I love sharing them with others.

I believe that a big part of hospitality consists of food: eating food, making food, sharing food. I am *not* an elaborate cook. Most things I make are very easy. Sometimes I have an occasion to make something special but we eat simply. Some of these recipes will be fast and easy, while others will take a little longer, but all of them will be yummy!

CHAPTER 7

Beginnings

"When you wake up in the morning, Pooh," said Piglet at last,
"what's the first thing you say to yourself?"
"What's for breakfast?" said Pooh. "What do you say, Piglet?"
"I say, I wonder what's going to happen exciting today?" said Piglet.
Pooh nodded thoughtfully. "It's the same thing," he said.
—A. A. Milne

"Doc" Maynard Pancakes

When I was a little girl, my Dad (nicknamed "Doc") would make our breakfast every morning. Living on a horse ranch we were always up early before school and would come in from chores to a warm breakfast. He usually used our electric griddle so he could make it all at once. It is odd for many of you to understand that it was a special treat for us to have cold cereal. We never bought it. My dad would buy it for a holiday. The package held a variety of different cereals individually packaged in little boxes lined with waxed paper so the milk would not leak out. I always wanted the frosted flakes.

When Dad made pancakes he always said the recipe out loud. I can hear it now: 2 cups flour, scant ⅔ cup sugar, north, south, east, west (4 tsps.) baking powder, dash salt, and so on. So, years later, when I was in my first apartment as I was making Dad's pancakes for the first time for Craig, the recipe came back to me as though I was hearing Dad recite it aloud. And I taught my kids the very same recipe. We would have our Doc Maynard breakfasts on Saturday mornings. Those were special times. We seldom went anywhere on Saturday mornings unless we had kids' sports or a conflict. Sometimes Craig would wake up and say, "Let's go out for breakfast!" But it was still "our time." Through the years, although we don't have the kids at home anymore, we still preserve our Saturday mornings. It is the only morning we have free together without rushing. Now Craig and I may take a long walk for coffee or tea and it is still a precious time.

"Doc" Maynard Pancakes

This recipe can also be used for waffles. The pancakes will be thin and not heavy. Many people who have told me they don't like pancakes have loved these because of that reason. Don't turn them over until the bubbles have popped. Enjoy!

2 cups flour
⅔ cup sugar
4 tsp. baking powder
dash of salt

2 cups milk
2 eggs
¼ cup vegetable oil

Mix all dry ingredients in a large mixing bowl with a wire whisk. Add milk and eggs, mix well. Mix in vegetable oil.

Spoon batter onto a heated griddle or frying pan. When most of the bubbles have popped, flip pancakes. Cook for an additional minute. Enjoy!

Best Ever French Toast

I don't buy special bread when I make French toast; I just use whatever I have on hand. I have included this recipe because of the spices I add to it. I just make it the way my family made it. It wasn't until I was an adult that I had someone else's French toast and decided it was very boring. Use stale bread for the best results. If you don't have stale bread, dry some out in the oven first or go buy some day-old bread—it really makes a difference because dry bread soaks up more flavor from the egg batter.

bread (however many slices you need)

eggs (I usually do about an egg per two slices)

milk (approximately a tablespoon per egg)

cinnamon

nutmeg

Preheat your griddle to the French toast setting or frying pan to medium high. Mix eggs and milk in a flat dish such as a quiche or pie plate. Then add spices. Take tongs and dip bread into mixture. Flip over to get both sides. Place on pan or griddle. Flip over after a minute or so. I usually add more spices to the egg mixture after dipping 3 or 4 slices to make sure there are enough spices on each slice.

When ready to eat, top with butter and syrup, berries, powdered sugar, or all of the above!

Lisa's Egg Strata

This dish should be assembled the night before. Such a great thing if you are having a lot of people over or you just do not have a lot of time in the morning. I have made this recipe for our family Christmas brunch in between stockings and gifts. My sister, Lisa, makes this quite often. She hosts many people at her lovely home. It is a great recipe for a large morning gathering. You can add salsa, veggies and different meats too! The word "strata" basically means a "layer," so you know it's gonna be deliciousness stacked on top of deliciousness!

Put bread cubes, sausage, and cheese into a 9 x 11" pan. Mix eggs, milk, salt and pepper, and dry mustard together. Pour over bread, sausage, and cheese. Cover and refrigerate overnight. The bread absorbs the fluid and looks like a soufflé. Bake uncovered for 40 minutes at 350 degrees Fahrenheit.

8 slices of bread cubed with crusts

1–2 cups shredded cheddar cheese

9 eggs, beaten

3 cups milk

1 sausage roll or package, cooked and drained
(you could also use cooked link sausage
cut into pieces)

Salt and pepper (to taste)

½ tsp. dry mustard

Mighty Muffins

Sometimes being welcoming means that someone may stop by at the last minute. They stay the night, and even though you are thrilled to have them, there needs to be food prepared: at least food for breakfast. You may not be able to run out to the store to buy something, but most of us have flour and sugar in our pantry. I decided muffins, no matter how basic, are something very easy to make at the last minute. They don't require a mixer or fancy ingredients. As a matter of fact, I chose two recipes to share with you that are easy to make, not necessarily because they are my favorites.

I chose the cinnamon muffins because they only require things most people have in their cupboard. I chose the blueberry ones because they are most people's favorite flavor. Even if you do not keep berries on hand, you can add something else to this recipe. I try to have berries, either fresh or frozen, on hand for health reasons and because I grew up in Washington, which overflows with berries.

Blueberry Muffins

2 cups blueberries
½ tsp. salt
1½ cups flour
2 tsps. baking powder
¾ cup granulated sugar
1 egg
1½ tsp. vanilla
⅓ cup vegetable oil
⅓ cup milk

Preheat oven to 375 degrees Fahrenheit. Spray muffin tin with cooking spray or use muffin liners. Mix together sugar, egg, oil, milk, and vanilla into a bowl. Add flour, baking powder, and salt. Stir together but do not overmix. Add in blueberries and carefully stir. Distribute into tin. Top with a tablespoon of sugar or coarse sanding sugar. Bake 25 minutes or until golden brown.

Cinnamon Streusel Muffins

¼ cup flour
1 tsp. baking powder
2 Tbsps. brown sugar
¾ tsp. ground cinnamon
¼ cup granulated sugar
¼ tsp. salt
1 egg
2 Tbsps. butter, melted
½ cup milk

TOPPING

¼ cup flour
2 Tbsps. brown sugar
¾ tsp. ground cinnamon
2 Tbsps. softened butter

Preheat oven to 350 degrees Fahrenheit. Spray muffin tin with cooking spray or use muffin liners. In a large bowl, combine flour, sugars, baking powder, cinnamon and salt. In a small bowl, whisk milk, egg, and melted butter until well blended. Mix together with dry ingredients only until moistened. Divide into muffin cups.

For topping, combine flour, sugar, and cinnamon. Cut in butter until crumbly. Sprinkle over muffins. Bake 15–18 minutes or until golden brown.

Scones

I had never even had a scone until I was over 30 years old. The first one I had was rather dry and I was not impressed, so I didn't try another for about 10 more years. It wasn't until I tasted a specialty scone that I started embracing the idea. Now I am hooked. The moral of the story: make good scones. I sort of morphed this recipe from a couple books. You can make so many variations so I had to pick two. I picked two of my favorites: Blueberry and White Chocolate Cranberry.

I know I said I don't make exact recipes. Forget I said that for a moment. You need to make this one fairly close to the recipe or it won't be right.

Happy scone making and when you bite into one you will be glad you took the time to make it. You can change the scones up by switching to strawberries, cinnamon, vanilla, orange cranberry, lemon poppyseed, and so on, limited only by your appetite's imagination! Enjoy!

Blueberry Scones

2 cups flour
1 Tbsp. baking powder
½ tsp. salt
2 Tbsps. sugar
5 Tbsps. unsalted butter cut into chunks
1 cup blueberries—fresh or frozen
1¼ cup heavy cream
sanding sugar for top
icing (optional)

Preheat oven to 400 degrees Fahrenheit. Mix together flour, baking powder, salt, and sugar. I usually take a wire whisk and stir dry ingredients. Then use a pastry blender to cut in butter. The mixture will look coarse, like flour-covered peas. Then use your hands to gently mix in your blueberries. Fold in your cream slowly until combined. Place your dough onto a lightly floured surface. Knead slightly and form into a round disc about 2 inches thick. I cut into 8 pie-slice-shaped pieces, then sprinkle with sanding sugar. Bake for 15–20 minutes. I make a thin icing with just powdered sugar and milk. I take a pastry brush and brush it on. Let cool.

White Chocolate Cranberry Scones

You can either add the white chocolate chips when you add the cranberries or add white chocolate icing to the top. The flavor will be different; I've done it both ways.

If you are aiming for a quick recipe, add white chocolate chips with the cranberries. This is a great addition to a Christmas brunch menu. It has a holiday flair to it, and these scones will fill your home with the welcoming scent of Christmas.

Christmas brunch is one of my favorite family gatherings. Christmas eve we go to our church candlelight service, then we sometimes look at Christmas lights on our way home and often read Luke chapter 2. Then, when everyone heads to bed, I fill the stockings. It is a magical time for me. The house is quiet. I sometimes read one of my many Christmas books and then set all the filled stockings in front of the fire.

We always told our kids, and now our grandkids, that they could open their stockings when they woke up, but we wait for presents until after breakfast. I always premade part of breakfast—an egg dish, fruit, and always some baked goods—so they wouldn't have to wait too long to open gifts. Memories of this precious time together warm my heart.

Follow the recipe for blueberry scones but replace the blueberries with ½ cup dried cranberries and ½ cup white chocolate chips. It is very sweet, so I do not always put icing on this recipe. Have fun adding different things to your scones!

Candy Cane Bread

For about thirty-five years, Re's family has been making candy cane bread at Christmas time to give to friends, family, and church leaders (and of course keep one themselves!). Her husband learned how to bake yeast breads from his grandma and in 4-H. Using Grandma Lil's 1970s-era Betty Crocker cookbook, he adapted this recipe. They use apple pie filling instead of the dried fruit. Their daughters have always decorated them with icing of many colors and candy sprinkles. The Candy Cane Breads were a bit messy looking when the girls were young, but just as delicious. Now their oldest daughter is the chief baker of the candy cane breads. As the girls got older, they took over the task of delivering all the breads, dropping them off and spending ½ hour to 1 hour visiting at a few select homes with the older people who receive them.

2 cups dairy sour cream

2 packages active dry yeast

½ cup warm water (105 to 115 degrees Fahrenheit)

¼ cup butter or margarine, softened

⅓ cup sugar

2 teaspoons salt

2 eggs

About 6 cups all-purpose flour (if using self-rising flour, omit salt)

1½ cups finely chopped dried apricots

1½ cups drained finely chopped maraschino cherries

Soft butter or margarine

THIN ICING

Blend 2 cups confectioners' sugar with about 2 Tbsp. water. If icing is too stiff, stir in a few drops of water.

Heat sour cream over low heat just until lukewarm. Dissolve yeast in warm water in a large bowl. Stir into water, the sour cream, butter, sugar, salt, eggs and 2 cups of the flour. Beat until smooth. Mix in enough remaining flour to make dough easy to handle.

Turn dough onto well-floured board; knead until smooth, about 10 minutes. Place in a greased bowl; turn greased side up. Cover; let rise in warm place until double, about 1 hour.

Heat oven to 375 degrees Fahrenheit. Punch down dough; divide into 3 equal parts. Roll each part into a 15 x 6" rectangle; place on greased baking sheet. With scissors, make 2-inch cuts at half-inch intervals on long sides of rectangles. Combine apricots and cherries; spread a third of the mixture down center of each rectangle. Crisscross strips over filling. Stretch dough to 22 inches. Curve to form cane. (Optional: let rise a second time before baking.)

Bake for 15–20 minutes or until golden brown. While warm, brush with butter and drizzle with thin icing. If desired, decorate with cherry halves or pieces.

CHAPTER 8

Tidbits

"Pull up a chair. Take a taste. Come join us. Life is so endlessly delicious."
—Ruth Reichl

The Relish Tray

When I was growing up we absolutely always had pickles, olives, carrots, celery and other tidbits for every holiday. Always. I just assumed that everyone else did too. When I got married I noticed that my husband's family had a few things I had never heard of, like those mini corns but they had a relish tray too. Through the years, I have realized not everyone grew up with this wonderful thing. I was pleased when Pinterest began an enormous section on relish trays, cheese plates, and so on.

I love the look of using all the wood cutting boards. I use some little china ramekins and tea cups. Use whatever you have on hand. I gather all sorts of fun treats, nuts, olives, crackers, sausage, fruits, and dips. My husband hosts work parties, and this has been a great thing to have out when people are gathering. Have fun with it!

The Relish Tray

Ingredients for this can be whatever you want, but I will include a list of things I usually like to have:

- a variety of cheeses, sliced or cubed
- sausage or other meats
- olives, Kalamata and/or black
- crackers, two types at least
- small chocolates
- nuts
- hummus and other dips
- grapes, two colors
- dried fruits

My Very Favorite Nut Mix

As a new administrator at the college I attended, I gleaned help from a few wonderful women. One of these dear ladies was the secretary to the college president and had been instrumental to my sister and I as students. She often had treats on her desk and always offered them to me when I stopped by for help on a project.

I was not a big fan of nuts at the time. We rarely had them growing up. She offered me a handful of her prized nut mix. Wow! What a wonderful thing. A bit salty, sweet, and tart—a great combo. You may look at this simple recipe and say, "I don't care for that ingredient," but before you go tweaking it, just try it. Let me point out that nobody who ever tasted liquid vanilla extract ever could believe it tasted so heavenly when mixed with other ingredients. Taste the mix before you shuffle the recipe—you'll thank me!

I have used this mix in care packages and have put it into small bags to add to a Christmas tray for a neighbor or friend. Friends say, "What was that? It's addictive!"

Mix together:

1 can mixed nuts
1 can butter toffee or glazed pecans or other nuts
1 package golden raisins

94

Grape Jelly Meatballs and Sauce

This tasty appetizer is from my friend Paul. The recipe was given to him way back when from his boss's wife. She made them for a company Christmas party and the meatballs were the hit of the evening. Ever after, these Grape Jelly Meatballs and Sauce have been a part of his holiday repertoire.

1 lb. hamburger
12 oz. chili sauce
6 oz. grape jelly (¾ cup)

1 tsp. salt
2 tsp. lemon juice

Make small 1-inch meatballs. Brown. Combine chili sauce, grape jelly, salt, and lemon juice in sauce pan. Heat. When mixture is well blended and hot, add meatballs. Remove from pan into warmer or crock pot.

Options:

1. 1 egg and ½ cup of smashed crackers can be added to the hamburger.
2. Mix ½ Italian sausage with the hamburger.
3. Turkey can be substituted for the hamburger.
4. Premade meatballs can be purchased from your local supermarket.
5. The meatballs can be cooked in an electric skillet at 200–250 degrees Fahrenheit, or in the oven at 350 degrees Fahrenheit for 30 min, in a deep casserole dish.

Several years ago, I was looking for some fun and easy new recipes for our Super Bowl party. I came across this one and have used it many times since. It takes just a short time to make and guests love it. I prefer it made with pepperoni but you can use sausage or ham. And I like to mix my Italian cheeses, too. It is a very flavorful appetizer or after-school snack.

Flavor-Packed Pizza Rolls

1 can Pillsbury pizza dough
1 small can tomato sauce
pepperoni, sausage or ham
1½ cup Italian cheese
    (I mix mozzarella and Parmesan)
garlic salt
Italian seasoning or oregano and basil

Preheat oven to 350 degrees Fahrenheit. Lightly grease two cake pans. Open can of dough and spread out on counter or board. Brush with tomato sauce, season to taste, and add meat and cheese. Roll up lengthwise. Cut into slices about 2 inches wide. Place into pans and sprinkle with cheese. Bake for 10–15 minutes or until golden brown.

Bruschetta

Whoever thought this up was genius. For centuries people have used their bread to sop up wonderful soups, sauces and gravies. The beauty of Bruschetta is that the bread generally has a crisp toasted texture and works perfectly as an appetizer. I have served with the topping separate from the bread or already topped for you. The photo I have chosen to represent this recipe was taken at my niece's wedding. It is a bit different than the one I use but I will give my recipe and tips from hers. Try this next time you are putting out appetizers for a gathering. It takes minutes to make and is so flavorful.

French baguette or other sturdy French
    or Italian bread
petite diced tomatoes or 1½ cup diced
    fresh tomatoes
1 Tbsp. olive oil
1 tsp. minced garlic
salt and pepper to taste
1 tsp. Italian seasoning or 2 tsps. fresh basil

½ cup mozzarella cheese
freshly grated Parmesan cheese
balsamic vinegar (optional)
or
top with ricotta, strawberries, mint, and
    tomato basil or peach balsamic
    vinegar

Cut baguette diagonally into ¼ inch slices. Lay out on cookie sheet. Broil just a minute or two until very slightly golden brown. Keep your eye on it! Remove from oven and add your topping. I add everything but the cheese and then top with the cheeses. Put back into oven and cook until cheese is melted and slightly browned. You can top with extra seasoning and drizzle some balsamic vinegar on it, if desired.

Although we often associate hospitality with women, my friend Susan's father-in-law loved to care for others with his cooking. From church potlucks to family barbeques, Bob's dishes were a coveted staple. His salsa was particularly amazing with home grown vegetables and there were never leftovers! Bob is now gone, but his children and grandchildren honor him by continuing to make his salsa.

Bob's Salsa

1 bunch green onions

1 medium onion

¼ Anaheim pepper

⅓ jalapeno pepper*

¾ tsp. garlic paste

3–4 Tbsp. ketchup

3 large tomatoes

salt and pepper to taste

Finely chop onions and peppers; combine in medium sized bowl. Stir in garlic, salt, pepper, and ketchup (this mixture can be covered and refrigerated for up to 24 hours before adding tomatoes and serving).

When ready to serve, dice tomatoes, remove the seeds, and drain briefly. Stir into onion and pepper mixture, adjusting seasonings as desired. Serve immediately.

*Note: this salsa recipe as written is mild. If you'd prefer more heat, increase the amount of jalapeno pepper.

Dips can be a wonderful addition to any party menu. I was recently at a Christmas party at my friend Jennifer's house. I absolutely loved this recipe. She said she found it on Pinterest but that's OK, all these recipes were from somewhere. I appreciated everything at her party. She even blocked off part of her garage and set up tables with craft projects. She had help from some other young women but it was a great example of someone utilizing the space they had to make a fun evening for a group of women to enjoy. Try this great recipe!

Artichoke Dip

8 ounces cream cheese

½ cup sour cream

½ cup mayonnaise

1¼ cup fresh Parmesan cheese, grated

1 8-ounce can non-marinated artichoke hearts, drained

1 dill weed, fresh or dried

1 clove garlic, crushed

Combine cream cheese, sour cream, mayo, and Parmesan cheese in a mixing bowl. Then stir in your artichoke hearts, garlic, and dill weed. Place the mixture in a baking dish, sprinkle with Parmesan cheese, and bake at 350 degrees Fahrenheit for about an hour. Serve with your favorite crackers or veggies.

Dilly Beans

My friend Lyn lives in the mountains. She cans a lot of their food. This recipe is one of her husband's favorites. Many times, when they have had people to their home or they go to someone else's, they bring a mason jar of these. Everyone raves about them, so I knew we had to add them to this book. They are a zippy addition to a relish tray with hardly any calories!

I think that when we welcome people into our home and lives, it is great to share some of our favorite things with them.

2 pounds small, tender green beans

1 tsp. red pepper

4 cloves garlic

4 large heads of dill

4 cups water

¼ cup salt

1 cup vinegar

Stem green beans and pack uniformly into clean, hot pint-size canning jars. To each pint, add ¼ tsp. red pepper, 1 clove garlic, 1 head dill. Heat together water, salt, and vinegar. Bring to a boil. Pour hot liquid over beans. Place lids and bands on at once. Process in a boiling water bath for 5 minutes. Remove jars from your canner. Makes four pints.

I am not a coffee drinker. I have tried and tried, but I just don't care for it. I am also not a big soda drinker. Years ago, I decided to mix some of my herbal teas to make sun tea. I loved the outcome. For probably about fifteen years, people have been asking for my recipe. I switch it up sometimes, but the basic parts stay the same. The nice thing is that since you are using herbal tea and it has flavor, you don't need any sweetener. I just make a large pitcher with this recipe.

Nicki's Iced Tea Blend

1 large bag decaffeinated black tea
1 bag Bigelow Orange and Spice Tea
1 bag Bigelow Plantation Mint Tea
1 bag green tea (optional, but it adds some healthiness, so I usually add it)

I sometimes change out a couple things: swap lemon for the orange, or use 2 big bags to make it stronger. But I most of the time, I use my regular recipe because people love it AND I never add sweetener of any kind. You don't need it with the mild flavor from the herbal teas. I used to always put my tea outside in the sun to make sun tea but now I usually just put it into a pitcher of hot water. Tea strength is individual preference. I like mine strong. I use a half gallon container most of the time but it really doesn't matter. Just watch it for how dark you like it. Remember, any good tea recipe can serve as the base for a punch recipe for any occasion.

109

Aunt Myrtle's Tea

When Ruthanne's husband's Norwegian aunt welcomed them in her home, they felt like they were being entertained by the queen, or at least a duchess. His Aunt Myrtle's delight was to serve guests delicious food on a beautiful table. One favorite treat was when she gave them special spicy tea in lovely china cups. Ruthanne keeps this mix on hand all winter long and serves it in cozy mugs—and sometimes china cups, of course. Why china cups? Because presentation can make it "more special."

Combine:

⅔ cup instant tea
18 oz. Tang
1 package of lemonade mix
1 tsp. cinnamon
½ tsp. cloves
1 cup sugar

Mix 1 Tbsp. of mixture into 1 cup hot water.

Hiram's Lemonade

This is my friend Re's father-in-law's recipe. He was a citrus farmer. Everyone loves this recipe and asks for it. It is on the sweet side, so you can reduce the sugar if you like your lemonade tart. The key is mixing the lemon juice and sugar together before adding the water.

1¼ cups of fresh lemon juice, strained (about 4–6 lemons)
2 cups of sugar
ice and water

Add 1 cup of sugar to the lemon juice in a one-gallon container. Stir together until sugar is dissolved. Add ice and water to make about one gallon. Add the other 1 cup of sugar (or less, to taste). Stir and serve cold.

CHAPTER 9

Salads and Sides

"After a good dinner one can forgive anybody, even one's own relations."
—Oscar Wilde

Moma Maynard's Potato Salad

I am sure that my version is a bit different than my mom's—and no doubt her version was different from her mom's, whose version was different from her mom's—but the basic idea and the key ingredients are the same. My sister uses the same ingredients as I do. Some say they don't love potato salad, but they love this.

6–8 medium size russet potatoes cut in half or quarters (depending on the potato), cooked
4 hard-boiled eggs diced into small pieces
¼ cup diced onion (optional)
3 sweet pickles, diced
approximately ½ cup mayonnaise
½ cup sweet pickle juice
1 Tbsp. Dijon mustard
garlic salt and pepper to taste
garnish top with some parsley and paprika

Add ingredients together. This is tough to write out, since I always make it to my taste, and if it looks too dry, I add more mayo or pickle juice. If I need a larger amount, I add more potatoes. Sometimes I use red potatoes. Have fun. Adjust to your taste. Try the original first to see what to adjust.

Quick Macaroni Salad

This is another family favorite and incredibly easy and quick to make. My kids have always loved this recipe, and when my son first got together with his wife, he told her she needed to learn how to make this. I wrote out the recipe and bought her a plastic salad bowl, hoping it would be fun for her. Once again, it's all in the ingredients. Make it with the tried and true ingredients first and then tweak if need be.

1 bag or box of salad macaroni
2 hard-boiled eggs, diced into small pieces
1 cup celery, diced
2 dill pickles, diced
¼ cup diced onion (optional)

½ cup mayonnaise
½ cup pickle juice
salt and pepper to taste
parsley (optional)

Cook macaroni as directed. Drain and cool. Mix macaroni with all ingredients. If it seems dry, add more mayo and pickle juice. Refrigerate.

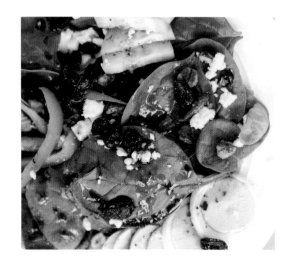

Dinner Party Spinach Salad

These instructions are based on an individual plate:

large handful of spinach

peeled and sliced cucumber

—about five slices

a few tomato wedges

sliced orange sweet pepper

feta cheese to sprinkle on

glazed pecans to sprinkle on

dried cranberries to sprinkle on

salad dressing (I use a sesame ginger

dressing or another sweet type)

This is very individual. You could also add bacon bits or olives—you are limited only by your appetite's imagination.

One of my reasons for writing this book and adding recipes to it was to inspire you and show you some quick and easy things to do when hosting others in your home. My daughter thought this special salad was essential to make a lovely dinner for special people.

You can make this in a bowl for a small group or your family but when I am hosting something special and this fits nicely with the other menu items, I put it on a salad plate. I carefully design it and it looks lovely and tastes even better. And as you are racing around getting things ready you can make one up as a sample and tell someone else to copy it. They will enjoy making it too.

I never had made this recipe until about five years ago. It is so yummy and now I love to make it in the summertime. It is extremely easy to make and is one of those items on your plate that just can mix with everything because it's almost like a salsa. As a matter of fact, I love it on top of a green salad. This salad is packed with flavor and requires no cooking, so it is a great thing to make on a hot day. So good. You can make it as spicy as you want or not spicy at all.

Corn and Bean Summer Salad

2 cans black beans, drained and rinsed

1½ cups corn: fresh, frozen, or canned

¼ cup red onion, minced

1 cup cucumber, peeled, sliced, and quartered

1 red bell pepper, diced (I often add another pepper like green or yellow)

1 avocado, peeled and diced (optional: I don't add it because I don't care for it—heresy, I know)

1 small can diced green chilies

⅓ cup cilantro leaves, chopped

DRESSING

⅓ cup olive oil

¼ cup lime juice

2 tsps. honey

1 tsp. chili powder

1 tsp. cumin

salt and pepper to taste

Cut and mix everything together. If you are adding avocados, add them at the last minute before serving. Then add dressing. Sometimes, if I am needing a quick salad to add to my menu, I just buy the honey-lime dressing, but you can make your own.

Julie's Cornbread

When I was growing up, I never cared much for cornbread. I thought it was too dry and felt it was obvious that everyone puts butter and honey on it to compensate for this. Then, when I had only been married a few years, I ate some of my friend Julie's and loved it. Yum! It was so moist, and I loved the texture. I asked for the recipe, and for the past thirty years, it has been the only recipe I've used. I asked if I could use her recipe for this book and she laughed and said it was not a secret recipe. I would not have found it without her, so we all call it Julie's Cornbread.

1⅓ cup baking mix

½ cup sugar

⅔ cup cornmeal

2 eggs

1 cup milk

¼ cup melted butter

Preheat oven to 425 degrees Fahrenheit. Mix dry ingredients together. In a separate bowl, beat eggs slightly. Add milk and butter. Combine liquids with dry ingredients, stirring only until moist.

Pour into greased 8 x 8" or 9 x 9" square pan. Bake for 20–25 minutes.

I must admit I love the entire process of making applesauce, from growing the tree until it's served up. For eighteen years, our yard included a small orchard. We had three apple trees, and as they got larger, they yielded more apples than I could handle. I would take every large container I owned, end up with them filled to overflowing and me looking for grocery bags, buckets, and anything that would hold apples and not give way under their weight. I had pots, baskets, bowls, bags. I would bring them into my kitchen, process the fruit, and do it all over again. There were so many apples that every year, I would tell a couple friends to come pick buckets for themselves.

I miss my trees. Several times, I've bought a lug of apples just so I could go through the process and have homemade applesauce. I had a system down. I would get out my biggest pot, put it on the stove, add about a cup of water, fill my sink with water, and vinegar (a great germ-killer) to put the apples in to clean them a bit, fill a large bowl with water and vinegar to put the cut apples in and set up my cutting board with my apple peeler/corer.

Then I would pick through the apples and fill the sink with about forty apples. I would cut them and put them in the bowl. Probably ten or so at a time. Then I would take them, scoop them up and put them into the pot and process until all gone. I'd add maybe ½ cup sugar and sometimes a little brown. I'd add about two teaspoons of cinnamon. I don't like it with too much, just a taste. I'd have the heat at about medium high, stirring occasionally. Add a bit more water if you need to; don't let it scorch. You may have to use a potato masher. They don't need to cook all the way down—just until the apples are soft. Then take a big spoon and put into your blender. Puree the apples until smooth. Pour into freezer containers. Best ever! And what's fun is to give this away to your neighbors or take to a friend.

Smooth and Sassy Applesauce

apples: I like to use Braeburn, Gravenstein, Gala,
  Golden Delicious, or Fuji
sugar: about a half cup for 12 apples
sometimes I add a couple tsps. brown sugar
approximately 2 tsps. cinnamon (to taste)
nutmeg (optional)

I take a large heavy pot and put in my peeled, sliced
and cored apples. I add about a ½ cup water. I cook
on medium high. It will get bubbly. Continue cooking
until apples are soft. Stir often but not continuously.
Add sugar and spices. Put into blender or food
processor. Blend until smooth. Put into freezer
containers or serve it up!

Some things I really like to keep simple, like Thanksgiving. Turkeys are easy. You put them in the oven while you're watching Macy's Parade, and it's just there … all day.

My pies are all made the day before. For lunch on Thanksgiving, I put out cheese, crackers, and fruit. I take my time setting the table and making it lovely. My girls like to help with this too. But then there is the crunch time. That hour and a half before it gets crazy. I get the stuffing ready for the oven and potatoes cooked. By then, Craig gets the turkey out to cool before he carves. And then I divvy out jobs: someone fill the water glasses and light the candles, someone make and stir the gravy, and so on. I am sure you have a holiday banquet preparation routine of your own. I am not sure how or when green beans were added, but they have become Thanksgiving dinner essentials. A couple years ago I wanted to switch things up and not have green beans, and my youngest said, "No! That's one of my favorite things at Thanksgiving!" I was thinking, *Really? It is such a simple thing, and not very special.* I guess it's the "heart" of the event. If hospitality can make green beans into an essential big deal, imagine what else it can transform? (We won't know until we get to Heaven.)

I have never personally really liked green bean casserole. I know many of you are scowling at me now. I just keep thinking, *Why do we need another high-calorie dish?* So, I take my wonderful, big, deep frying pan and put in the fresh green beans (not canned!) and put some olive oil, salt, pepper, paprika, and maybe some bacon or almonds, flip a few times, and they are done. Sometimes I add a tablespoon of butter for flavor, but not always. It also frees up room in your oven for any things that need to be warmed at the last minute.

Green Beans Perfecto

as many beans as you need
salt and pepper
paprika
onions (optional)

bacon (optional)
sliced almonds (optional)
olive oil

Heat large skillet. I use my deep sided one. I sauté onions and bacon first then I put beans and seasonings into a large bowl and coat with olive oil. Then cook in frying pan, stir frequently until beans are tender but not overcooked. If you add the almonds, I like to brown them a bit, so I add them partway through cooking the beans.

This is another one of those easy recipes to feed a group where you can do the prep ahead and stick it in the oven an hour before while you work on other details. They look pretty and taste yummy and complement almost any food.

Oven Potatoes

small sized red and golden potatoes
olive oil—enough to coat potatoes
garlic salt and pepper to taste
paprika—enough to sprinkle on top
Italian seasoning or oregano and basil

Preheat oven to 350 degrees Fahrenheit. Mix
potatoes and olive oil in large bowl. Add seasonings.
Mix well. Pour out onto a deep cookie sheet or
broiler pan. Bake for about 1 hour 15 minutes.
Brush with melted butter before serving if desired.

CHAPTER 10

Main Courses

*"Hospitality is not about visual or culinary pleasantness
but about helping hearts connect."*
—Unknown

BBQ Pork Tenderloin

pork tenderloin

olive oil

garlic salt and pepper

dried parsley

paprika

Rub tenderloin with olive oil. Sprinkle all over with garlic salt, pepper, parsley, and paprika. Barbeque about 45 minutes and baste with a sweet barbeque sauce.

Alternatively, you can bake it in the oven. Preheat oven to 350 degrees Fahrenheit. Bake for about an hour.

Let cooked meat rest for at least 5 minutes (10 minutes is even better) and then slice and serve.

If there is one meal that people always say to me, "What is this?" it is pork tenderloin. I have made it for our family, small groups, and have taken it as a meal for someone. I never had it growing up or even in my early married years. I think I discovered it about fifteen years ago. I love it so much I will eat it for breakfast the next morning. It usually comes in two pieces. and makes enough for about 6–8, depending on your guests.

It is extremely easy to make and there is no real "official" recipe; because it is so delectable and always a great hit with my guests I decided to include it—it is a genuine treat (and makes for incredible sandwiches if you have any leftovers). We "usually" cook it on the barbeque to make that nice barbeque flavor but in the winter, I just cook it in the oven. Don't overcook, but make sure to cook it enough, since it is pork. That is the only thing that may be difficult. I usually put garlic salt and pepper on the outside. Sometimes paprika. Then just cook. When it is mostly cooked, I put a sweet and tangy barbeque sauce on the outside. Make sure that you wait a couple minutes before cutting to allow the juices to settle on the inside—if you cut too soon, they will all ooze out, and you will end up with a dry pork loin.

135

My sister-in-law, Moe, makes the best pot roast. She tells a few of her secrets to making it taste so good: "This is a meal that takes a while to cook. My personal preference is low and slow. Use Johnny's garlic seasoning mix. This should be in everyone's kitchen at all times. I have a fresh large jug of it. I can never run out. Use as much garlic as you want. I never use less than a whole handful; it's how I roll. My grandson, Marley, and I feel it will protect us from any vampire or zombie apocalypse that might occur."

About the broth: "You will want to just drink this broth from a goblet because it's so, so yummy! You have three options for your broth:

1. Heat and leave as broth and ladle it over your selection of meat and veggies in individual shallow wide bowls, add some mayo horseradish, and swirl it into your meal.
2. Make yummy gravy by throwing some butter into your empty roaster pan. Once you remove the meat and veggies, put it on your stove top, add flour, lightly brown it up, then gently and slowly add in your broth. Cook a few minutes until thickened. Place your meat and veggies on a deep-dish plate and smother it all in gravy.
3. Or have both options because my family loves both!

"If you feel you need a side dish, cornbread with jalapeño is great or some biscuits. Your gravy will be burgundy in color. And your meat will appear burnt, when cooked right to perfection. You're welcome!"

Moe's Pot Roast

3–5 pound chuck roast (get an extra-large roast because you can never have enough leftovers)

salt and pepper, to taste

Johnny's garlic spread and seasoning

1 cup of good, tasty red wine

about 3 cups beef broth

2 Knorr beef bouillon cubes

4–5 garlic cloves, peeled (or more!)

red potatoes, halved or quartered, depending on size

2 onions, quartered

6–8 carrots, whole or halved

mushrooms (optional)

rutabagas, or any other root veggies you happen to love

2 Tbsps. butter

horseradish

Preheat oven to 275 degrees Fahrenheit. Season roast with salt, pepper, and Johnny's garlic seasoning. Place in a roaster pan. Pour red wine and beef broth over it. Add beef bouillon cubes to liquid.

Peel and quarter all vegetables, set aside. Place the discarded ends from the vegetables and the butter into the broth in the pot. Cover roast and cook until meat does not quite pull apart (about 2 hours for a 3-pound roast, and 3 hours for a 5-pound roast).

Remove meat from the pot and strain broth. Place meat back into pot with a couple of ladles of the broth to cover the bottom of the pan. Reserve the rest of the broth. Add in potatoes, onions, carrots, mushrooms, and any other vegetables you want. Cover and cook for about one more hour, or until vegetables are done and meat is falling apart.

Serve with broth (au jus) or use broth to make yummy gravy.

Flavorful Meatloaf

2 pounds lean ground beef
1 egg
bread crumbs or oatmeal
    (about 1 cup)
garlic salt and pepper

½ cup barbeque sauce
1 cup ketchup or tomato sauce
3 tsp. Worcestershire sauce
onions (optional—I do not add)
cheddar cheese (optional)

When I first got married, I made a couple dishes that caused my husband to ask what they were—not because he did not like them, but because they were so unlike anything he'd had before. Families make things differently. His mom was a great cook, but this isn't how she made meatloaf. This isn't exactly how my Moma made it, either. I tweaked it a bit. You can formulate your own version; a meatloaf recipe is whatever the chef decides it is. It's fun to experiment! One of the greatest joys in the kitchen is creating the exact list of ingredients you like.

This recipe can be changed to your preference. I use what I have on hand. Preheat oven to 350 degrees Fahrenheit. I mold the sides with my hands in a shallow baking dish. Mix the ground beef with egg and bread crumbs or oatmeal. Add other ingredients (except for cheese). See if it is the right consistency. If the mix is too wet, it won't hold together. Add a little more of the breadcrumbs or oatmeal if needed. After the loaf is formed, add a little barbeque sauce and some cheese on top. Bake for an hour or an hour and a half.

138

Moma's Baked Chicken

This was one of the first recipes I learned to make for dinner. I was cooking dinner for our family at a young age. Moma would show us how to make certain things, then we would make them from then on. I have changed this recipe a bit through the years and am sure that it is not exactly like the original. It is such an easy thing to do for a group, and although it is so simple and common, it was requested by a few people when I was choosing recipes for this book.

as much chicken as you need
    for your gathering
½ cup milk
½ cup flour

¼ cup Parmesan
1 tsp. paprika
salt and pepper to taste, but probably
    a tsp. of each

Preheat oven to 350 degrees Fahrenheit. This recipe is very individual. I use my broiler pan, cover it with foil, and make slits in it.

Pour milk into a shallow bowl to dip chicken. Take a gallon-sized bag and add dry ingredients. I don't measure these out. I just put some flour, Parmesan, and lots of spices into bag. Dip chicken into milk. Place chicken (no more than two pieces at a time) into bag and shake until covered. Place onto pan.

Bake for 1 hour to 1 hour 15 minutes. I usually bake top side up and turn over before the last half hour.

Aunt Betty's Lasagna

1–2 pounds mild Italian sausage (I use ground sausage, but you can take the meat out of casings if you need to)

uncooked lasagna noodles (not quite a whole package)

2 medium sized cans tomato sauce

1 can tomato paste

1 can diced tomatoes

1 Tbsp. minced garlic

1 tsp. basil

1 tsp. oregano

1 tsp. parsley

¼ cup diced onion

mushrooms or peppers or other veggies (optional)

salt and pepper to taste

1 large container ricotta cheese

1 16-ounce bag shredded mozzarella cheese

fresh Parmesan cheese for top

Preheat oven to 350 degrees Fahrenheit. I make my sauce first. Brown the sausage, onions, and whatever vegetables you add to your marinara sauce. Then add all your tomato sauce, tomato paste, and diced tomatoes. Add seasonings. Let cook on low for at least 30 minutes. Put some sauce on the bottom of a baking dish. I use a 9 x 11" pan, but it can be whatever size you want. Layer half of the uncooked noodles, ricotta, mozzarella, and sauce, repeat. Make sure you end with sauce on top. I admit that sometimes I need extra sauce; keep an extra small can of tomato sauce on hand just in case. Add a bit more mozzarella and then cover with foil. Bake for 50 minutes, then uncover. Sprinkle with Parmesan and cook for 10 more minutes uncovered. Remove from the oven and let it sit for 10 minutes before cutting.

Tuna Roll-Ups

This recipe was given to me by my friend Ruthanne. She tells her story: When I was a freshman at Western Baptist Bible College in El Cerrito, CA (Now Corban University, Salem, OR), a single missionary lady, Jenny Adams, spoke to our dorm women. She told us, "You will always be expected to serve people food, everywhere you live, so learn to make something that tastes good, and always have those ingredients on hand." That advice stuck with me, and I chose this recipe from my mother. We liked it as kids, and I served it hundreds of times to my family and to drop-ins through the years. In fact, once a traveling group of singers from one of the colleges landed unexpectedly at our house at dinner time. Surprise! That was the time I served 8 guests plus the 4 in our family with 3 cans of tuna fish! Well, we did have a few other sides to go with it, but still…

1 can of tuna, drained   ¼ cup celery, finely diced

1 hard-boiled egg, chopped   peas, cooked in sauce (optional)

Mix 1 can tuna with egg and diced celery. Spread on biscuit dough. Roll up like a jelly roll and slice. Bake at 400 degrees Fahrenheit until slightly brown, about 12 minutes. To serve, top with white sauce and peas.

BAKING POWDER BISCUITS

2 cups flour   2 Tbsps. shortening

4 tsps. baking powder   ¾ cup milk

½ tsp. salt

Blend dry ingredients and shortnening with pastry blender until crumbly. Stir in milk just to moisten. Pat out on floured board. Cut. Bake at 400 degrees Fahrenheit until slightly brown.

WHITE OR BÉCHAMEL SAUCE

2 Tbsps. butter   1 tsp. white pepper to taste

2 Tbsps. flour   (black is OK)

1 tsp. salt or to taste   1 cup milk

Melt butter in a saucepan over low heat, use a wire whisk to stir in flour, salt and pepper. Stir constantly for about 2 minutes; do not brown. Gradually stir in milk and continue cooking over low heat, constantly stirring until sauce begins to thicken. For a richer sauce, add a couple teaspoons of heavy cream.

Easy Tamale Pie

This is not the traditional recipe because I developed this when my kids were little and I needed some easy recipes. My oldest daughter loves this recipe and makes it for her family now.

2 pounds ground beef or chicken
taco seasoning (to taste)
1 can black or pinto beans (drained
        and rinsed)
1 bag frozen corn
1 can diced tomatoes

1 small can diced green chilies
2 cups shredded cheddar jack cheese.
tortilla chips
black olives (optional)
sour cream (optional)
salsa (optional)

Preheat oven to 350 degrees Fahrenheit. Brown meat (drain if needed) and add taco seasoning. Mix seasoned meat with beans, corn, tomatoes, and green chilies in a bowl. Add extra salsa if you want it spicier. Take a large baking dish and put a layer of crushed chips on the bottom, meat mixture, then 1 cup of the cheese. Do this twice. Top with more crushed chips. Bake for 30 minutes. Top with olives and sour cream.

Quesadilla Casserole

This is one of those recipes that's super easy and cheap, and you most likely have the ingredients. You could add meat if you wish, but the whole point is to be able to make it super quick. I like it with a bit of sour cream on top when I serve it.

6–8 flour tortillas, medium size
cheddar jack cheese mix
1 can diced tomatoes
1 can diced green chilies
sliced black olives for the top

Preheat oven to 325 degrees Fahrenheit. Grease baking dish lightly. Put about a ¼ cup of cheese in each tortilla and sprinkle with green chilies. Roll up and repeat until pan is full almost to the brim. Pour tomatoes on top, making sure everything is covered. Sprinkle on a little more cheese and add olives. Bake for 20–25 minutes. Serve with sour cream if desired.

Everyone has their own chili recipe. I have a couple different ones—some easier than others, and some spicier, too. I actually really love chili. I take a flour tortilla, tear it into fourths, spoon some chili into it, fold it, and eat it that way. I love it. Here is the recipe that I make for a large group. It is not overly spicy and has some shortcuts, but you need to make it in the morning and put into your crock pot or Dutch oven so the flavors combine.

My Chili

1 large can chili beans

1 large can kidney beans

1 can black beans

1 can diced green chilies

1 can diced tomatoes

about a cup of your favorite salsa

1 small yellow onion diced

1 package Italian sausage or
    ground beef

garlic salt and pepper to taste

4 Tbsps. chili powder

Brown meat and onions. Add spices and chilies. Add remaining ingredients. Put into crock pot. Cook on low for a few hours. You are just keeping it warm so there is no exact time frame. Top with cheese.

P.S. Chili is always better the next day. Make extra so you have leftovers!

Easy-Schmeazy Taco Stew

This is the easiest recipe, and I love it so much. I found it years ago in a magazine of some sort. This recipe has been such a blessing to me. It is a great throw-together recipe. Yum!

3–4 boneless chicken breasts

1 can black beans, rinsed

1 can pinto beans, rinsed

1 can diced tomatoes

1 can diced green chilies

½ cup salsa

1 bag frozen corn

2 cups cheddar cheese

tortilla strips or chips

sour cream (optional)

Put chicken breasts in bottom of crockpot. Add beans, tomatoes, chilies, and salsa. Let that cook for about 6 hours. Just leave for the day. I prefer to cook on high for the first 2 hours and then turn to low. Take two forks and shred the chicken while it's in the pot. Add corn about 30–45 min before serving. Add cheese about 10 minutes before serving. Top with tortilla strips, and maybe some sour cream.

CHAPTER 11

Sweet Endings

"We elves try to stick to the 4 main food groups:
candy, candy canes,
candy corns and syrup."
—Buddy the Elf

Some of my very favorite recipes come from the recipe compilations of a church, community group, or family. There you will find the tried and true recipes that have been tested over time by the contributors' family and friends and on likely each other at potlucks, picnics, funerals, and socials. I have a couple of these soft-cover spiral-bound cookbooks chock full of all sorts of wonderful things which are basically everybody's best recipes.

Such is the case with this simple, tasty cookie bar recipe that follows. Couldn't tell you where it came from, but I do know that after making it for the past twenty-five years, I claim it as "mine." It is quick and fairly easy to make when you lack the time or energy to make something more elaborate. Just be sure you make plenty and save a few back for yourself for later as people always exclaim over how much they love it. "Oh my goodness! What IS this?" as they eat the last cookies on the platter.

Some people have a recipe like this called Magic Cookie Bars or Seven-Layer Cookies. It is very similar. I have not made those but they are probably wonderful too. I recently looked up Hello Dollies on Pinterest to see if they did in fact exist under that name, and I did find them. Most were the same, or maybe a little bit different. I usually have all these ingredients on hand, except maybe the milk. Make these soon and enjoy them!

So, whose grandma really invented this recipe? Who knows and who cares? But if you ask my grandkids they will tell you I did!

Hello Dollies

1 cup graham cracker crumbs

¾ cup (6 Tbsps.) butter

1 cup coconut

1 cup chocolate chips

1 cup finely chopped pecans

1 can sweetened condensed milk

Preheat oven to 375 degrees Fahrenheit. Melt butter and add to graham cracker crumbs. Mix together and press into a square 8 x 8" pan. Add in the following order: coconut, chocolate chips, pecans. Then cover with sweetened condensed milk. Bake for 20–30 minutes. Cool before cutting.

Anna Mae's Peanut Butter Cookies

My Grandma Anna Mae died when I was fourteen. She was a creative, thoughtful, industrious woman. She taught my sister, Lisa, and me to cook and sew. She was always creating. One of the things I fondly remember was her making peanut butter cookies, wrapping them in a long tube of wax paper, and refrigerating them. Then she would cut them in slices. Then we would roll into a ball, take forks, and do the crosses on top.

There is nothing dramatic about these cookies. You too have most likely done this, but I needed to include it, since it was a memory for me and demonstrates how important something so simple can be for a child. This is a wonderful tradition for your kids and grandkids. This recipe is easy for little ones, and a great way to help them start baking.

1¼ cups peanut butter
½ cup shortening
1¼ cups light brown sugar,
      packed
3 Tbsps. milk
1 Tbsp. vanilla extract
1 egg
1¾ cup flour
¾ tsp. salt
¾ tsp. baking soda

Preheat oven to 375 degrees Fahrenheit. Cream together peanut butter, shortening, brown sugar, milk, and vanilla, mixing well. Add the egg and beat until blended. In separate bowl sift together flour, salt, and baking soda. Slowly add to creamed mixture until blended.

Shape into a long tube and roll in wax paper. Refrigerate. Bring out and slice whenever you wish. Roll into balls. Crisscross with fork dipped in flour to prevent sticking. You can just bake a few at a time if you wish.

Bake for 8 minutes and cool on cookie sheet for 2 minutes before moving to wire cooling rack. Do not overbake.

Serve with milk, a napkin, and a smile.

Ranger Cookies were one of the first cookies I ever tried at my in-laws' house. At first glance, I thought they were just a chocolate chip cookie, but after tasting one, I discovered how crunchy it was. Yum! It just has corn flakes added to an oatmeal base.
Who knew?

Judy's Ranger Cookies

2 cups butter or margarine
2 cups brown sugar
2 cups granulated sugar
4 eggs
2 tsps. vanilla
2 cups oatmeal

2 cups corn flakes
4 cups flour
2 tsps. baking soda
1½ cups raisins or
     chocolate chips

Preheat oven to 350 degrees Fahrenheit. Blend together butter and sugars. Add in eggs and vanilla. Stir together dry ingredients in a separate bowl. Mix dry ingredients with butter/sugar mixture and then add chips or raisins. Drop by tablespoons onto baking sheet. Bake for 12 minutes.

Fudge Meltaways

½ cup butter

1 square unsweetened chocolate (1 oz.)

¼ cup granulated sugar

2 tsps. vanilla (divided)

1 egg, beaten

2 cups graham cracker crumbs

1 cup coconut

½ cup chopped nuts

¼ cup butter

1 Tbsp. milk or cream

2 cups sifted confectioners' sugar

1½ squares unsweetened chocolate
   (1½ oz.)

Melt ½ cup butter and 1 square of chocolate in saucepan. Blend granulated sugar, 1 tsp. vanilla, egg, crumbs, coconut, and nuts into butter-chocolate mixture. Mix well and press into well-greased baking dish: 11½ x 7½" or square 9 x 9" pan. Refrigerate.

Mix ¼ cup butter, milk, confectioners' sugar, and 1 tsp. vanilla. Spread over crumb mixture. Chill.

Melt 1½ squares of chocolate and spread over chilled filling. Chill. *Cut before firm*. Makes 3–4 dozen squares.

This recipe is not baked but has three layers to refrigerate. Although it is not complicated, you must allow enough time for the fudge to set. My Moma had an old Betty Crocker cookie book. Due to some complications in our home, I was the delegated baker ever since I was about eleven or twelve. As an artist and as a very visual person, I would look at the cover over and over, read thru the book and pick things I thought looked interesting.

Years later I discovered that my mother-in-law also had the very same book! When I told her I grew up using it, she dug hers out and handed it to me. So, I have a copy, my sister has a copy, and I learned that my best friend also has the copy her mom used. I have been trying to find copies for my kids and grandkids. The copyright is 1963 and I hear it is still available.

This recipe is in the special cookie section in the back. I don't think I realized when I began making them that they would end up being a special holiday treat when I grew up and had a family. This is the recipe that three people in my family request at Christmastime. Follow the recipe closely so they turn out perfect. I feel confident they will become a requested holiday favorite of your family, too.

Dick's Peanut Brittle

Here is another recipe from Susan that originated with her father. Hospitality toward others can take many different forms. Since the early 1960s, her dad has been making his addictive peanut brittle every Christmas to share with friends and family. Although now retired, he delivered countless boxes of the fresh candy to his coworkers over the years. Here is Dick's famous recipe along with personal tips for success.

1 cup light corn syrup
2 cups granulated sugar
½ cup water
2 cups raw Spanish peanuts (with skins)

1½ Tbsps. butter
1½ tsps. vanilla extract
2 tsps. baking soda

Butter two large sheet pans with sides and set aside. Prepare clean countertop or table area to spread out peanut brittle after cooking.

In a heavy saucepan, combine corn syrup, sugar, and water. Cook slowly over medium heat, stirring occasionally with a wooden spoon. When candy reaches about 230–240 degrees Fahrenheit, begin to add peanuts, sprinkling in slowly (over about 15 minutes) in order to avoid dropping the temperature. Continue to cook and occasionally stir until candy reaches 300 degrees Fahrenheit. Remove from heat.

Working quickly, stir in butter and vanilla, then add baking soda and stir again. Quickly pour into prepared pans and spread out with a spatula.

Let peanut brittle rest in pans for a few minutes until center is slightly cooler, then flip each pan (one at a time) onto prepared work surface and using two forks, spread out to desired thickness (my dad likes it as thin as possible). The candy will still be very hot to the touch at this point.

Cool completely and break into pieces, storing in an airtight container.

Tip: Use a large heavy pan and a good, accurate candy thermometer. Keep the heat steady and cook slowly. Don't be tempted to turn up the heat to speed up the process. The last 5–10 minutes of cooking go very quickly, so watch the thermometer carefully. Try to avoid making candy on a humid day, but if you must, increase the final temperature by 1–2 degrees Fahrenheit.

Fantasy Fudge

My sister-in-law, Diana, made this recipe for many years as a special gift to give friends and family. You may have made this recipe yourself. I know I did years ago for Christmas each year. The special thing about this is the fact that she was making a special treat that was appreciated by the recipients. It is an example to all of us that no treat is too basic to be enjoyed by those you know and love.

3 cups sugar
¾ cup butter or margarine
1 small can (5 oz.) evaporated milk
    (about ⅔ cup) (Do not use
    sweetened condensed milk.)

3 pkg. (4 oz. each) BAKER'S Semi-Sweet
    Chocolate, chopped
1 jar (7 oz.) marshmallow creme
1 cup chopped walnuts (optional)
1 tsp. vanilla

Line a 9-inch square pan with foil, with ends of foil extending over sides. Bring sugar, butter and evaporated milk to full rolling boil in 3-quart saucepan on medium heat, stirring constantly. Cook for 4 minutes or until candy thermometer reaches 234 degrees Fahrenheit, stirring constantly. Remove from heat.

Add chocolate and marshmallow creme; stir until melted. Add nuts and vanilla; mix well.

Pour into prepared pan; spread to cover bottom of pan. Cool completely. Use foil handles to lift fudge from pan before cutting into 1-inch squares.

Sue's Blackberry Cobbler

This is my personal favorite recipe. It's at least tied for first with "Doc" Maynard's Pancakes. Growing up on a horse ranch in Western Washington with 3,000 feet of riverfront along the Pilchuck River, one must pick berries. Lots and lots of berries. We probably have acres of blackberries on our property. As kids, we would pick and eat them or the birds just got them. I think Moma froze them for winter but rarely did we have dessert made from them.

My sister moved up into my grandparents' home years ago and her mother-in-law gave her an easy cobbler recipe to utilize those berries. I got the recipe years ago and have made it for all sorts of gatherings. You can switch out the fruit or buy frozen berries in the winter. It doesn't matter how or what you use, but *make this recipe!*

Sue's
Blackberry Cobbler

1 cup flour
¾ cup sugar
¼ tsp. salt
1½ tsps. baking powder
¾ cup milk
about 4 cups berries, washed and drained

Preheat oven to 350 degrees Fahrenheit. Put a spoonful of flour and sugar into berries and turn into pan. I have used differently sized pans and adjusted the batter, but this is generally done in a 9 x 13" pan. I have also used this same recipe with peaches or apples. Mix other ingredients together. Spoon batter over berries. Bake for 45 minutes or so. Serve with vanilla ice cream or fresh whipped cream.

The Berry Pie

And sometimes it really is about the pie! I was not actually going to add this recipe, but this pie was in a lot of our photos and ended up on the cover! Then someone told me they could hardly wait to make it … uh oh. So I'm going to share the easiest way of making this pie. You can make it more complicated, but I will share how I made the one on the cover. Have fun!

1 package double crust pie dough
1 bag frozen mixed berries (4 cups),
    partially thawed
1 Tbsp. lemon juice
½ cup flour

¾ cup sugar
dash of salt
½ tsp. cinnamon
2 Tbsps. butter

Preheat oven to 400 degrees Fahrenheit. Put berries into a large bowl ahead of time so they can be mostly thawed, add lemon juice. In a smaller bowl, mix flour, sugar, salt, and cinnamon. Mix dry ingredients with berries.

Put bottom crust into pie pan, add filling. Dot top with butter. Add top crust and crimp edges. Make slits in top.

I usually take a pastry brush and lightly brush with water then sprinkle sugar on top. Place foil around edges.

Bake for 40 minutes or until golden brown.

Spiced-Up Pumpkin Pie

I remember my Moma making her pumpkin pies the day before Thanksgiving. She would just make the Libby's recipe on the can's label and add the usual spices and then add nutmeg on top, and sometimes finely chopped walnuts. I am not a walnut fan, so I never cared for it that much. As I got older, I realized that I actually love anything pumpkin; I just don't like walnuts. So sometimes I will add pecans to mine, but usually I don't add nuts.

So why then do people tell me all the time that they don't usually like pumpkin pie but they like mine? This greatly confused me since it's such a basic recipe, but I have heard this for years. The only thing I can figure is because of the nutmeg. Perhaps that is the key. I actually use fresh grated nutmeg. Nine years ago, my husband and I went on an anniversary cruise and one of the stops was Grenada, the Spice Island. We went on a tour of a spice plantation. Oh, my! The smells were fabulous. And then, of course, you can purchase spices. I brought back all sorts of things, including nutmeg. You crack open the shell and then there is a nut inside. You can buy a spice grater or just use the very finest on your hand-held cheese grater. After the pie is made you add to the top. I can smell it now.

Spiced-Up Pumpkin Pie

1 cup granulated sugar
½ tsp. salt
1 tsp. ground cinnamon
½ tsp. ground ginger
¼ tsp. ground cloves
2 large eggs
1 can pure pumpkin (15 oz.)
1 can evaporated milk (12 oz.)
nutmeg (optional)
pie crust: basic dough or refrigerated pie dough

Mix together sugar, salt, cinnamon, ginger, and cloves in a small bowl. Beat eggs in large bowl. Stir in pumpkin and sugar-spice mixture. Gradually stir in evaporated milk. Pour into pie shell. Grate nutmeg over pie. Bake in a preheated 425-degree oven for 15 minutes. Reduce temperature to 350 degrees Fahrenheit; bake for 40–50 minutes or until knife inserted near center comes out clean. Cool on wire rack for 2 hours and then refrigerate.

Lisa's Southern Lemon Cake

Years ago, our small Bible study group met in the home of a couple who lived near us. He was a Montana mountain man and she was an Alabama southern belle. She is so dear to me. She would come home from church, put on her pink Auburn sweats, and still have her pearls on. I'd go home from her house and find myself talking with her soft twang. She still is the classic representation of southern charm and hospitality. Before Bible study, we would have supper, as she called it. On several occasions, Lisa made her lemon cake. Oh my goodness gracious! I had never tasted anything like it. Today you can find it on Pinterest; I believe it is called lemon jello cake. This is a perfect summer barbeque dessert to make for a large group.

1 box lemon cake mix
1 small box lemon jello mix
4 eggs
¾ cup water
¾ cup oil

GLAZE

2 cups powdered sugar
½ cup lemon juice
    or more to taste

Preheat oven to 350 degrees Fahrenheit. Grease and flour pan. Combine cake ingredients and mix together. Pour into prepared 9 x 13" pan. Bake 27–30 minutes. Prepare glaze while cake is in oven. Prick cake with fork all over and pour glaze onto cake while hot.

Triple-Layer Chocolate Cake

Sometimes, during difficult times, a special homemade treat is a great encouragement and pick-me-up. When my friend Susan was experiencing a difficult pregnancy years ago, many lovely friends surrounded her with their gracious hospitality: sending roses, praying, and cooking or baking for her family. One particularly memorable dessert was a homemade chocolate cake with chocolate frosting that they devoured despite their grief at the probability of losing their baby. This story has the perfect ending: that baby is now a young woman of twenty-five, and here is the recipe for the best homemade chocolate cake you'll ever eat (recipe credit: *Taste of Home*).

Triple-Layer Chocolate Cake

CAKE

1 cup butter, softened

3 cups packed brown sugar

4 eggs

2 tsps. vanilla extract

2⅔ cup all-purpose flour

¾ cup baking cocoa

3 tsps. baking soda

½ tsp. salt

1⅓ cups sour cream

1⅓ cups boiling water

FROSTING

½ cup butter, cubed

3 oz. unsweetened chocolate, chopped

3 oz. semisweet chocolate, chopped

5 cups confectioners' sugar

1 cup (8 oz.) sour cream

2 tsps. vanilla extract

Preheat oven to 350 degrees Fahrenheit. Grease and flour three 9-inch round cake pans.

In a large bowl, cream butter and brown sugar until light and fluffy. Add eggs, one at a time, beating well after each addition. Beat in the vanilla extract.

In another large bowl, whisk flour, cocoa, baking soda, and salt; add to creamed mixture alternating with sour cream, beating well after each addition. Stir in boiling water.

Transfer batter to prepared baking pans. Bake for 30–35 minutes or until a toothpick inserted in center comes out clean. Cool cakes in pans for 10 minutes. Remove from pans to wire racks to cool completely.

In a metal bowl over simmering water, melt butter, unsweetened chocolate, and semisweet chocolate, stirring until smooth. Cool slightly.

In a bowl, combine confectioners' sugar, sour cream, and vanilla extract. Add the melted chocolate mixture and beat until smooth. Spread frosting between layers and over top and sides of cake. Refrigerate leftover cake.

PART 3

The Little Details— Extra Fun with Easy Home Ideas

"That boy is your company. And if he
wants to eat up that tablecloth,
you let him, you hear?"
—Harper Lee

CHAPTER 12

The Welcoming Entry

*"May all who enter as guests
leave as friends."*
—Unknown

People approach your entry every day. It may just be you or a family member but someone does. Your entryway greets them and introduces you, whether it is a porch or just a door. You also have a sidewalk usually to follow. Maybe you have landscaping on either side. Whatever your home is like, you have a door. In my current home, I may have the cutest entry I have ever had. I was so excited about it when we moved here. It was the thing that made me fall in love with this house. It has a porch that wraps around three sides.

I didn't love the color of the house, shutters, or door, but I knew I could eventually change the color palette. For right now, the simple thing was to just paint the front door. The house is white with black shutters and had a red door. The door was in bad shape. Craig painted it a cobalt blue. I love it. It doesn't really hide the dents in the door, but down the line, we may just replace it. You can get small cans of paint to do doors, and it is a quick fix.

I wasted no time finding a couple of cute chairs and accessories for this porch. I can hang flower baskets and such. I have always been a person who had a wreath on my door, no matter the season. From January to August, I usually have a basic one that just goes with the house. Then in September to November, I have a fall one, and then in December, a Christmas one.

Sometimes in fall and Christmas time I have garland around the door or another porch decor. I don't always do the same thing but I always do it inexpensively and don't replace things every year. I may add one new item, if need be, to spruce something up, but it is not about fancy; it's about welcoming. I think front doors are a big deal!

I also believe that what you feel as you enter a home is important. Some homes have entryways and some homes you walk right into a room. Whatever kind of entry you have, make it special. Usually I have a rug, and maybe a little table. Then people can set things down, or perhaps a little chair or bench where they can put shoes on and take them off. Sometimes key hooks are helpful, and I always have a mirror of some sort so people can take a look if need be. Whatever your living situation, however small or large, whatever shape house, people walk into a space and instantly get a feel for your home. Make it count.

Some houses do not have front porches. Or maybe they have a back porch or sunroom. My wonderful porch on my current home gave me great ideas that formulated in my artistic head. I have implemented some but not all of these ideas. I also have a pergola that covers my back patio. It is old and needs some work but has wisteria growing over it which gives it much of its charm—it's calendar pretty!

Even in homes that do not have porches, I know people sit outside in chairs. Sometimes you can add flower pots, rugs, and outdoor art. The idea is to make a cozy space that welcomes family, neighbors, and friends. Conversation is a great facilitator of hospitality.

189

BUILDING A WREATH

The easiest and quickest way to make a basic wreath is to begin with a form. I will use a grapevine wreath for this example.

Gather your supplies. I use a variety of shapes and sizes of flowers and greenery. Keep in mind what season or color scheme you want your end product to reflect.

I have all my pieces cut into the right size and ready to just fit them in. I usually fit all of one type in at a time so that it is spaced out around the wreath. You may need to trim the stem of whatever you are using. I sometimes have to use my glue gun. For this example, I am just fitting each piece into the form of the grapevine.

As you hang your wreath, you may see that it is lacking in an area and need to readjust it a bit. No worries; just tweak it.

Voila!

CHAPTER 13

Inside Warmth

"There is an emanation from the heart in genuine hospitality which cannot be described, but is immediately felt and puts the stranger at once at ease."
—Washington Irving

Home interior design is limited only by our imaginations and our pocketbooks. The possibilities of interior decoration inside our homes are endless and can be unique to each of us. There are so many nuances, styles, and decoration options for setting up one's home. There are hundreds of books and magazines on the subject addressing every topic, inside and out, so that is not my ambition here. One of the purposes of this book is to inspire the reader to greater expression of hospitality, in every way, with a special emphasis on home entertainment. I think the main takeaway from this book regarding having a "warm" home should involve the following:

- where you usually meet with guests
- your guest bathroom, even if it's the only one
- a guest room for sleeping
- your kitchen
- your dining/eating area
- outdoor spaces

First impressions count! When I know guests are coming, I always check the bathrooms to ensure that the porcelain is sparkling, the trash can is emptied, the room smells good, and my decorative towels look pretty. The kitchen, which is likely to be somewhat messed up if there has been any cooking or food preparation, needs to look spotless or at minimum like a kitchen on a TV cooking show, with the sink and preparation areas clean. If the trash can is full, it needs emptying. Ideally, you'd have something yummy in the oven or coffee brewing or maybe a candle to give off a homey feeling. I'm not going to tell you

how to clean your house, but remember how you primped for your first date, or a big social event—take as much care to make sure your house looks as good for your guests as you can within the time available. I know this book is entitled *It's Not About the Pie*, meaning things don't have to be perfect but they can be clean.

You can do so much with your eating area very simply and quickly. When I am hosting a dinner party for Craig's work friends, I plan differently than when we just have a few friends over or when it's a family gathering. Buffet style is less formal and easier to pull off than a formal Sunday dinner setting. It's good to think things through and have a back-up plan, just in case.

It sounds basic, but it's essential: when we have a Bible study group in our home, I need to make sure we have enough chairs. I always have a few folding chairs in case we need extras. I also have a couple of folding tables in case I need them (and those folding tables and extra chairs can be used outdoors, too).

My dining area is used to the max. There is nothing I enjoy more than to sit around a table and share life with others. It is one of my favorite parts to my home. It is where you share food and stories, where you share your heart.

We all need to have a restroom for guests to use. You may only have one bathroom in your home. That is OK. Make sure it is clean and presentable. If you have a powder bath, then you can stock that more for guests.

When you have guests spend the night, make sure you show them where the towels are and make sure if they have not brought with them what they need, that you help them figure it out. Have a spare toothbrush or comb. I use a washcloth. I can't tell you the number of times through the years when I have stayed with people and have not been offered a washcloth. I can make do, but it is nice to have one.

You may have a guest bedroom or maybe you have a pullout sofa. Whatever the case for your guests, get their bed ready for them. Make sure they have enough blankets. I usually leave the stove light or another small light on in case they need to get up at night. I also show them where the plugs are for their phone or laptop.

If your guests have arrived late and are not familiar with your home, show them where glasses are for water and let them know if your water is OK to drink from the tap.

I usually mention the morning schedule: if someone is leaving for work, when they will get in the shower, and where there is breakfast food if everyone is going out for the day.

Bottom line: Try to introduce your guests to places in your home they may need to use so they do not feel awkward and instead feel right at home. Most guests won't want to put you out, so try to think of things so they do not have to ask you.

CHAPTER 14

The Setting of the Table

"There are times when wisdom cannot be changed in chambers of parliament or the halls of academia but at the unpretentious setting of the kitchen table."
—E. A. Bucchianeri

You may be setting your table for a fancy dinner party, an outside picnic, or just a cup of coffee with a friend. How we set our table creates a welcoming atmosphere. It sets the tone and it makes people feel special.

If you are using linens, begin with a tablecloth. I use all sorts. I don't just use plastic tablecloths outside; sometimes I use cloth. I am a firm believer in using everything I have and not just "saving" nice things for special occasions. Every day is a special occasion, and I love to just make it pretty.

I usually place some sort of topper over the top of the cloth. Fabric napkins are a wonderful thing. I use them in my home for so many things, from lining a bread basket to covering an end table or using them as a topper.

I utilize any greens that are abundant in my yard and cut pieces.

I choose candlesticks or vases or wooden boxes and then just lay greens around them.

Set your table. I have the melamine dishes for outside so there is no breakage. We have pets and kids who have little toes that can be injured.

I hope you see the vision that you can use whatever you have available. You can use your good dishes (I don't think they should be hidden away but used) or your everyday, even plastic or paper. Grab a candle from another room, a tablecloth, or a cloth napkin. Just something simple to make your table special for your special guests.

CHAPTER 15

Your Outside Space

"I think that I shall never see
a poem lovely as a tree.
A tree whose hungry mouth is prest
Against the earth's sweet flowing breast;
A tree that looks at God all day,
And lifts her leafy arms to pray;
A tree that may in summer wear
A nest of robins in her hair;
Upon whose bosom snow has lain;
Who intimately lives with the rain.
Poems are made by fools like me,
But only God can make a tree."
—Joyce Kilmer

I am definitely an outside girl. Growing up on a farm with riverfront, tall cottonwoods, and a gorgeous view, I think I was a little spoiled. Being outside gives me a sense of peace and calm. That was then and this is now. I have a very small yard now, but I go outside, sit in my chair, and enjoy the start of the day with God and my chocolate Labrador Retriever. And if it's cold, I just have a mug of hot tea. It doesn't matter how cold; I still go outside (and my Lab loves the cold mornings!).

Backyards are where family gathers and friends come for barbeques. They are where children play and pets romp. Even with the smallest of porches, it is the gathering place. When we were in an apartment we still sat out there in the evening. I much prefer enjoying the outdoors conversing over the insect noises and watching the stars come out over being in the house. When we used to host large groups at our previous home, I would concentrate on flowerbeds and the porches. One of my friends asked if I needed to do anything inside before a gathering. Huh, I hadn't even thought of it. I was so excited to be outside.

I am just going to show you a couple ideas for your outdoor space that may encourage you. I have learned to utilize the space I have from small to large. We don't need to have the biggest or best. You learn to use what God has given you even if it is a 350-square-foot duplex. And just think, once you master the 350-square-foot duplex, you will have great fun taking what you've learned and applying it in a bigger venue. It will be like when you were little and graduated from the small box of crayons to the really big one!

Insects need not be a problem for you outdoors. You can get plants that insects avoid, special lights, candles, or even a bug zapper if you're into hearing the flying pests sizzle. Birds will keep the insects away. I have some beautiful birdhouses made by a friend that totally beautify my backyard. He has been making birdhouses for years. Some are small to hang on a tree, and some are large enough to house multiple bird families. He also tells you how high to put them and how to take care of them.

I love his philosophy of birdhouses:

> "What could make you feel better about your backyard than to have birds that visit frequently? A backyard that is welcoming to our feathered friends is a wonderful thing. Who doesn't smile when they hear a bird singing, or baby birds chirping while waiting for their parents to feed them. Having "birdhouses," or as some like to call them, "nesting boxes," is an excellent way

205

to make your backyard feel welcome to many species of birds, friends and family."

Here is a quote from *The New Birdhouse Book* by Leslie Garisto, which supports this idea:

"A birdhouse symbolizes all virtues of home—safety, enclosure, stability, and functionality. When we put a bird in a cage, we are exercising our dominion over it.

But, when we set out a birdhouse, we acknowledge that our lawns, gardens, and back yards can never belong to us alone. Each birdhouse erected represents not just the survival of a pair of birds but an opportunity to reproduce and increase the species. It is a simple way of repaying the birds for their countless gifts to us."

Another quote from Abram L. Urban says it all: "Poor indeed is the garden in which birds find no home."

CHAPTER 16

Events on a Dime

"Before everything else, getting ready is the secret to success."
—Henry Ford

For over four decades, I have been involved with decorating and planning social events, starting when I was just a teen. Sometimes I had large budgets but usually have not had much of a budget, yet I worked to make each event not just a success but a memorable occasion that people enjoyed. I have always just done what I could to make something sparkle. I am an artist but being an artist is not necessary to pull off a great event. I do believe I learned most of what I know about hospitality through time, and trial and error. I hope to give you a couple guidelines to help you with your special function coming up, whether wedding, graduation party, family event, church banquet, or a child's birthday party.

Primarily, you need help; someone you can count on to be relied upon. Ideally, you might have a person or people in your life already who are like that. For me, my sister, Lisa, is one such person. We have done so many events together that we hardly have to even talk while we are doing it. We know how we operate and what our individual gifts are and so that makes it easy. My daughter Emily is another such person God has blessed me with. Emily is a whirlwind of energy. She can make anything beautiful, whether it is making 180 custom cupcakes from scratch for a wedding or taking an old piece of junk and repurposing it. All my kids are actually great workers at events. Maybe it is because their mom dragged them along to help when they were young. Hmm, it would be interesting to hear their perspective on this subject. Now I'm in trouble: I've started listing people and I know I'm going to leave someone out and will be apologizing until my next book is written so I can mention them there!

Seriously, I have many close friends that I have worked with on events as well. My best friend, Susan, has always been an inspiration to me and we have worked fast and sometimes frantic on a project. I appreciate those people in my life who have come to my rescue when I got in over my head. I would say, "Yes, I will do that for you," when I shouldn't. I think it is good to sacrifice, but I also think we cannot do a good job if we are overextended.

If someone comes to you and needs you to help with an event but they can only spend a very minimal amount, that is a major compliment. They know you have skills to do a great event and that you can do it better for less. When that happens, here are a few ideas to help.

We have a lot of events at our church. Sometimes we have fifteen tables set up, and sometimes thirty. Doing centerpieces is always a priority. Something you can do quickly and inexpensively. This is true of reception areas for weddings also.

You can use so many things and not all tables have to be the same. As a matter of fact, I like it better if they aren't. Here are some steps:

- Use tablecloths (matching, or scatter your colors).
- I usually use a topper like a cloth napkin or a runner. You could also use a wood piece or straw mat. We even used nautical maps at one event.
- Then you want your main feature like candles, flowers, leaves, balloons, lantern or other decor items.

A couple from our church recently made wooden boxes—many wooden boxes. They are amazing, and we have used them for so many events. Here are some ideas that can inspire you and would not cost you much to do for your event.

215

PART 4

Hospitality Comes in All Shapes and Sizes

*"Hospitality is love in action.
Hospitality is the flesh and bones of love."*
—Alexander Strauch

CHAPTER 17

The Pilchuck Family Farm

"Stories are verbal acts of hospitality."
—Eugene H. Peterson

When I was six, we moved to Snohomish, Washington, a little town 35 miles north of Seattle. We had about thirty-five acres and 3,100 feet of riverfront property along the Pilchuck River. We moved from Woodinville, where we had a small number of horses that my dad was training. My mom and dad would go to horse shows and trail rides on weekends. My dad had a day job, but his passion was horses. So, he was in his element when we got more land in a beautiful location. Our home was a converted chicken coop: long and narrow, with many windows on only one side. It had a door at each end and a carport connecting to the barn. My mom was a city girl. She enjoyed the horses, but I think this house was not necessarily her dream. She embraced it and never complained. However, she didn't really want to entertain there. My dad died when I was thirteen. We had no income and had to sell most of our horses the month after his death. Times were very hard. No improvements would be made on our property for many years.

Through the years, Moma moved past her insecurities and out of the depression that had engulfed her for many years. She died at 97. The last twenty-five years of her life were her happiest, and in her final years, people would come sit in front of her rocker and thank her for faithfully praying for them and their family members. She spent hours in prayer each day. Her Bible and her Corrie Ten Boom book were her close companions. She always had a plate of cookies on the table to give her guests.

About thirty years before she passed, my sister, Lisa, and her husband, Sam, moved to the farm from their home in Northern California. The three of us had gone up for a visit one summer and found that people had trashed our beach with dirty diapers and broken glass bottles. The people renting our grandparents' house had not paid rent for several months. Sam said, "We are moving up here next month." Lisa was a nurse and found a job right away. They kicked out the people in our grandparents' home and moved in. Then the process began. In the barn, there were piles of tools mixed with chicken poop and toys. It was not an easy task to clean up. There were repairs needed in both houses. There were acres and acres of blackberries that had taken over. You seriously felt that you may have to helicopter in if more time were to pass. Slowly, very slowly the farm began to shine like it never had before. Sam loved construction and cut out three windows on the north side of Moma's house. That in itself brightened Moma's outlook. Having Sam and Lisa come live there gave her encouragement and as her grandbabies were born, it helped Moma to come out of her sometimes-depressed state.

She returned to church, made friends and decided to host an outside spaghetti dinner for her retiree group every August until her final year. This was a testament to my sister who did most of the work and planning. Which brings us to an entire new part to the story.

My sister and husband have opened their home and property up to others for the past thirty years. With its park-like setting, many ask to come with their families to

camp, swim and have bonfires. Sam mows several acres and it is really an amazing destination. There is a trail for horses, pedestrians, and bikes that flanks part of the property. There is also a great spot for floating on the river and the farm is only 45 minutes to the San Juan Islands or Seattle. The past several summers they have had guests every weekend for three months. They are amazing hosts and reach out to those who need respite.

Sometimes we need to be open and available to people. Do we know someone who needs a night out? Maybe someone with small children or special needs. Maybe we need to give up our Friday night date night for time with a friend who is struggling with life. This is a hard one for me. I appreciate my time on Friday nights with my husband. That's why sometimes it is a sacrifice. Some people do not even get that luxury to go out at all. Movie or sports tickets are another great idea.

Our church has mail folders, for everyone. We used to have boxes but we grew too big and needed the space and now have file folders. I love this! It is so easy to write someone a note or put cash in an envelope and slip into their folder. At Christmas, it is a special treat to be able to do Christmas cards for everyone and put them in the folders. If we did not have these we would only mail to a few. It is an easy way to bring joy to people. Sometimes there are even little gifts in the folders.

My sister also ministers to those who are sick. She is a nurse who goes beyond the norm. She continually visits the sick and calls to let them know she cares and lends an understanding ear. I have no clue about medical things and it is hard for me to be empathetic when I do not understand but I think we can all listen to people. Sometimes that is all someone needs.

Not all of us have acreage to share with groups, but we can use our porch, backyard, kitchen table, or living room to invite a friend over to visit over coffee or tea. It does not need to be fancy or in need of a special dessert. Just something simple and a warm smile.

CHAPTER 18

Wonderful Examples to Follow

"Follow my example, as I follow the example of Christ. I praise you for remembering me in everything and for holding to the traditions just as I passed them on to you."
—1 Corinthians 11:1–2 (NIV)

We can probably all remember amazing people in our lives who ministered to us when we most needed it. People who warmed our heart and reached out to make us feel welcomed and included. Maybe someone who didn't even know you. Sometimes it was not convenient for them, and maybe it was financially difficult, as well. I have many people who have helped me through the years. I think sometimes I wasn't even aware the impact they would have on me until many years later.

When my dad died, I was a teen. We had no income, so I was not able to go a lot of places. We also had chores to do. After Dad passed, we began going to a little country church. They invited Lisa and me to youth group and we immediately plugged in. What a blessing it was to belong and to be able to feel a part of this group. If we had no transportation to get to an event, someone would take us. Time and time again, people came to get us so we could take part in the fun activities. We had "after game parties" after football games. Our pastor and wife lived two blocks from the high school, and every time there was a home game, we would go to their house. We planned skits and games. We had treats and such fun times.

It was one of these times that our pastor's wife, Ruthanne, was making pizza dough. This was fascinating to me since I had hardly ever had pizza let alone homemade pizza. I asked if I could help, and she said, "If you ask, I will put you to work because I will take you at your word." That has stuck with me for years. We need to be genuine in helping others.

When we ask someone at church how they are, are we prepared to listen or do we inwardly roll our eyes? And when someone asks us, do we just say "fine," even if we aren't? We need to accept help from others too. If others do not see us as "real" then how can we minister to them? We are not perfect and should not come across that way. Honesty in times of genuine hurt or distress makes being puffed up with pride impossible.

Later when we were in high school Pastor Darrell and Ruthanne moved to Idaho. Twenty-five years after that, my husband, Craig, transferred his job to Idaho, and we went to their church. We have had many years under their ministry. Ruthanne always has a pot of tea and cookies or scones to share. I know I can call them in any emergency. They have always treated me like a daughter, and that means more to me than they know.

Because they treat me like a daughter, they also know they can count on me, too. One time they called upon me to meet a need that some, myself included, may not feel able or qualified to do. They had plans one evening, and an emergency came up that needed attention. There was a man from out of state who had a heart attack and was in the hospital. His wife had come, but the pastor of their church in Washington had called Pastor Darrell to meet her at the hospital. So, he asked if I could go meet her, and then they would come as soon as they were able.

Uh … ok. So I headed to the hospital. When I got there, I saw the blue light by the CCU (Cardiac Care Unit) door: a code. Yes, it is true. He had died. I had not even yet met this woman, and now her husband had passed. I was able to meet with her and our senior adult pastor. Awhile later, Pastor and Ruthanne arrived. The woman's husband had been living in a small trailer. It was decided that the woman, Pam, would come home with me. I phoned Craig and told him. We made up our hide a bed and as I pulled away from the hospital, Pastor and Ruthanne waved to me with reassuring smiles of comfort. The next day I took her to the funeral home and the trailer. Then she had relatives come.

This was out of my comfort zone for sure, but I would want someone to reach out for me in the same situation if it were me. It was not important that I felt uncomfortable. In some small way, I could help someone else.

The summer of 1977 was a very busy and exciting time. I had just graduated from high school and Lisa was going to come home from college to marry Sam. They were coming home a couple weeks early to help Moma with fixing up the house and farm for company. No one had much money, but we could spruce things up a little. The wedding was to be at our church in July, but the reception would be outside at the farm. Lisa would also have some of her friends coming early to help.

This was all pretty unnerving for my mom. She was trying to re-cover furniture, and I was making curtains just to try to make it look presentable. The Saturday before the wedding, a group of men came from our little church. They had roofing material and planned on re-roofing our home. I was super stoked. Moma was fuming. She said it was like a slap in the face. I wasn't even sure what she meant. I just knew that someone was helping us. Hooray! Sam told his new mother-in-law that she needed to let the body of Christ work. She let them work and then raced around to see if we had any food to give them for lunch.

I was young and was not in on the planning of this, but these men knew the conditions we lived in. They knew Moma needed help, and they wanted to meet that need. They gave money and supplies to help a widow in need. They sacrificed their time and energy. This is what can happen if people put their minds together to help others. It is difficult for many of us to allow others to help us, but we need to be willing to allow it. Maybe you can't do it on your own, but you can get a couple of friends together to do it with you.

James 1:27 tells us, "Pure and undefiled religion in the sight of our God and Father is this: to visit orphans and widows in their distress, and to keep oneself unstained by the world."

A college friend, Cathy, was widowed just a few years ago. She shared with me how friends and loved ones can help.

> After my husband of thirty-three years passed away suddenly, one of my hardest social hurdles to cross was figuring out where I stood as a widow in our friend group of couples. Dickson and I had a well-established group of friends who loved celebrating life events

together. We enjoyed movies, dinners, game nights, birthdays and random adventures. After Dickson passed, I was not sure how I fit into that couples-based world. I am happy to say that, even though I was tempted to decline the first few invitations, I have been convinced by each of them that I am still a much loved and enjoyed part of our friend group. I have also been convinced that if I were not with them they would have lost two friends not just one.

My encouragement to you is to include and remember your dear ones who have suffered loss. Allow them to continue to enjoy life with you and don't be afraid to talk about their loved one. Share freely what you miss about them, and how that person's life made a positive impact on yours. I have a friend who frequently will just say, "I am missing my friend today." When others feel comfortable sharing their feelings with me, it allows me the freedom to share with them when I have some feelings that need to be shared.

Over the course of my life, I have had some wonderful examples of genuine hospitality. Often it's the little things that make a gigantic difference. Here's a few instances where a determination to be hospitable made a difference in people's lives.

My friends Neal and Patti sacrifice their time and energy every Sunday by hosting our church's large group of university students in their home after church for dinner. They feed them and let them just hang out in their home rather than being in a dorm room all weekend. Nothing beats a home-cooked meal! There are hours of time given in food preparation and home cleaning; I am sure sometimes they are exhausted but they continue to faithfully care for these young people and pray for them—it is their ministry, welcoming these young adults away from home and family into their home (and it probably is an answer to the students' parents' prayers, too). What a continuing great outreach of hospitality and Christian love: being there every week, for every student, making sure each of them knows they have a home away from home. No activities really need to be planned; just loving on them is enough.

Another example: When my daughter Jessica was in college, she was driving her little car on her way to a camp to work for the summer, and the car caught on fire on the freeway. She was a long way from a town of any size. We ended up calling my friend, Re, who had AAA. They sent a tow truck, and Re drove over an hour to pick Jessica up. She then took her home for the evening, fed her dinner, let her spend the night, and then drove another hour the next day to take her to meet up with her best friend in Fresno. Her friend's mom then drove an hour to take them both to camp the following day. No one balked at any of this. No one was frustrated with the sacrifices. They just jumped in and served. No questions asked. This is what it's all about, folks. Jesus said it this way: "Treat others the same way you want them to treat you" (Luke 6:31).

For over two decades, a family friend has invited people to their home for Christmas dinner, sharing food and sometimes a Christmas movie: something for them to feel they have had a special day. The idea is that you are cared about, that you matter. Such hospitality doesn't have to be fancy or expensive—just a genuine heartfelt sharing of what the Lord gives you and bringing joy to another's life.

Hospitality can change lives for a lifetime. Re told me another story about a man who had started attending their church by the name of Dave. Dave had been institutionalized as a child because he had been diagnosed to be of low mental capacity; he also had a mouthful of rotten teeth. He could have been mistaken for being homeless, but he was not. He lived in a rundown one-room hotel room. Somehow one day Dave started attending their church and soon ended up attending the Bible study in their house, and also the Life Group they also hosted. Dave, as a direct result of their Christian hospitality, grew into a more whole personality and due to fellowship, his walk with Jesus grew. They became his surrogate family as he had no loving family nearby and over the years they spent hundreds of hours together sharing meals and God's love with him. But the story does not stop there: Dave had a friend named Gary who lived in the same rundown hotel as he did. Gary was different than Dave in that he had no interest in church and refused to talk about Jesus or God, but he would ask for and accept a ride to the grocery store, or various food items, or a ride to his doctor's office. God kept bringing the reclusive, hurting soul that was Gary across their path. He could be rough, grumpy, and demanding, but he desperately needed the Christian love and Good Samaritan–type assistance they provided him and ended up eating Easter dinners with them. Gary wouldn't talk about God, but through Cliff and Re showing Christian hospitality, Gary saw God's love in action. Their families might have forgotten Dave and Gary, but God had not, and thus with plates of food, deliveries of groceries, and rides to the doctor they experienced unconditional love and Christian community. Don't scoff—Gary saw them loving Dave, and as much as he might not want to have admitted it, Gary wanted to be loved and to feel like he mattered, too.

It needs to be said: God often answers prayers through our Christian brothers and sisters. There are so many ways to give to people. I cannot even begin to scratch the surface of ideas. I was thinking of some small things in my life that were very big things at the time. I remember Pastor Darrell and Ruthanne coming to my college for a meeting he had. I visited briefly with them and mentioned that I was busy while they were there with classes and work. I also mentioned that I had to hem my dress for chorale, the music group I was in, and we were singing the next day. When I finally got back to my dorm room later that day I discovered my dress hanging on my closet door, hemmed. She never told me she was doing it. She never asked which room or dorm. She used her resources and figured it out. I don't even know where she got the needle and thread, but it was the biggest blessing to me. I was amazed.

Another time in college I had a bill for an odd amount, like $59.48 that was overdue. I reached into my purse later that day and discovered an envelope with the exact amount. And I don't think I ever told anyone. But what is amazing about that is that it showed me that God had my back because *He knew.* He knows every detail and every need.

The Bible tells us to do these things in secret, but sometimes there is a need you need to help with and it is immediate, so you just need to do it. The recipient may know it is you. I think it is a heart issue. You are not doing it for the recognition; you are doing it because you know it's a need and you want to help.

CHAPTER 19

The Easter Dress

"Respect people who find time for you in their busy schedule…but love people who never look at their schedule when you need them."
—Unknown

Mardell, my roommate from my sophomore year in college, sent me a paper she had written while finishing her degree at another university. She had moved home to Washington to get her credentials to teach English. She sent me this paper because I am mentioned in it. I asked her if I could use it because it fits this book so well. It is an example of someone helping someone out when it was least convenient and having a heart of hospitality.

As an English teacher, she was mortified that I would use an unedited college paper and has revised it slightly, but the majority of it remains the same.

THE EASTER DRESS

Mardell Mickels Gill

"You study too much," Nicki said, dropping a cascade of textbooks and a binder on her bed. She had found me at my desk with pen and highlighter in hand amidst my own papers and books.

"No, I don't," I stubbornly replied to her regular exhortation. "Actually, I don't study enough." Nicki rolled her eyes, sighed, picked up her gear, and headed for the gym where she worked evenings as a trainer for women's sports. In the quiet of our dorm room, I continued analyzing English literature and memorizing notes for Russian history.

Throughout the first semester of our sophomore year, Nicki would often interrupt my moments of bookishness, saying, "Mardell, studies aren't everything,"

"I know, Nicki, but I am at school to study, so it must be my priority."

"But not everything you need to learn for life is in books," she countered.

I know, I know, I thought, *but I'll learn the other stuff later*. Nonetheless, Nicki's words lingered in my mind as I continued my study habits, sometimes skipping Sunday evening services at church and most social activities. I tried to ignore the pained expression that often shadowed her face as she would leave the room.

Second semester began in January, and the realization that I had only four and a half more months at Los Angeles Baptist College disturbed me. I would be returning twelve hundred miles to my home state of Washington to earn my degree, and I didn't want my friendships to dissolve across the distance. Determined to strengthen my relationships, I took a lighter load of classes and spent more time with my friends. Occasionally, I would study in the lounge, engaging in conversations between intermittent reading and notetaking. Needless to say, my studies suffered a little, but I was discovering that I could sacrifice a few points of my GPA to develop a more balanced personal life.

As winter was eclipsed by spring, I was more comfortable with my new approach of reaching out to others, including offering help in editing papers for other students or typing up a project for a friend. I was not clinging to every minute of study time in fear that it wouldn't be enough. Learning to depend on the Lord for guidance in time management, I was finding peace in discovering God's definition of "enough."

Easter weekend significantly furthered my pivot. On Saturday afternoon, our bubbly, blond freshman neighbor Robin was still laboring away on her Easter dress, the iron steaming and the sewing machine humming away. Robin had not had very much experience in sewing, so Nicki and I were advising her on garment construction. Robin had had the dress fabric for over a week, but between classes and homework, it took five days to pin the pattern onto the fabric and two days to cut out the pieces, with actual construction beginning on Friday afternoon. Nicki and I gently impressed upon her that she must hurry a bit or she wouldn't get the dress done in time. Robin was making progress slowly when suddenly she remembered she had committed to babysitting for a family that evening. She'd have to finish the dress when she got back later that night.

Reclining on my bed with my chunky Norton Anthology balanced against my knees, I was pondering some English poetry, but my mind kept drifting to the earlier scene of Robin struggling along. Calculating her progress, I realized there was no way Robin would finish her dress in time. Excitedly, I dropped my book and whisked into Robin's room to play fairy godmother. When Nicki found me a couple of hours later, she beamed. Robin came home at two o'clock in the morning, surprised and overjoyed to find me in her dimly lit room with a nearly completed dress in my lap. She would have her brand-new Easter dress for the next morning, just like all of her Easters when she lived at home with her family.

The Easter dress plunged me toward a change in my self-image. Rather than simply developing myself as a scholar, I began a journey of trusting the Lord to guide my responses in sharing time or money to help others. Spending the rest of my undergraduate years at Central Washington University, I determined to pursue both scholarship and Christian community in the secular environment.

A few years later in graduate school, I realized that Jesus had accomplished much in my heart. Having banked good grades over my first quarters of study, I was able to set a lower mark for my last two classes, confident that my GPA would be very respectable even if I let my grades slip just a bit. I was able to balance academics and ministry that summer, enjoying the opportunity to sing with a traveling music group, weekly ministering in parks and prisons. Notwithstanding the heavy load of reading, researching and writing, I cultivated new friendships while sharing the Gospel.

Life is a constant sorting of priorities, and often the Easter dress comes to mind. As a wife, a homeschooling mom, and a servant at church, I've been balancing needs in disparate areas. I've continued to monitor expectations and rotate attention. Within the day-to-day march of demands, there sometimes arises a divine distraction—a coffee date with one of my own collegiate daughters, a walk with a friend in the park, a weekend to spend with my mom four hours away. Long ago, a new pattern was stitched into my life. Now, rather than treasuring duty over destiny, I eagerly grasp the fleeting moments that could easily slip away.

This story may not make you automatically think about hospitality but it is about going out of your comfort zone to help a neighbor—maybe next door in a dorm—but a neighbor. Mardell did not have to leave the comfort of her room and her books and study time. But she was prompted in her heart to reach out to another young woman in such a way that it brought great joy to someone. And I bet Robin still remembers that gesture of kindness when someone went far beyond what they needed to do.

CHAPTER 20

Extend Grace

"For He will deliver the needy when he cries for help, the afflicted also, and him who has no helper. He will have compassion on the poor and needy, and the lives of the needy He will save."
—Psalm 72:12–13

Psalm 72 is a coronation psalm written by Solomon. It describes the time when God, King over all, will reign and all classes of society will live in harmony (if only). We started this book with a definition of compassion. What is it truly, and how do we embrace it? We may say that we care for others and that we care about the poor but are we *doers*? I know that I fail at this. There are so many ways we can reach out and help. I have always wanted to do disaster relief but that has not worked out, yet. I have other lofty goals, but sometimes we need to just do the simple things that are around us: volunteer our time, work at the rescue mission, fill Operation Christmas Child boxes, visit the elderly, take a meal to a neighbor, provide Christmas gifts to kids who won't get any, and so on. There are so many ways that are right in front of us.

A friend relates her story about an unlikely friend she made who ended up blessing her socks off.

> We have had a number of friends that were on the fringe of society. It was not always easy taking the time to meet their needs or to include them in our life, but God placed them in our path for years. Joanne was a former drug addict, tattooed from head to toe (before tattoos became common for the general populace), had lost all her kids to foster care, and then got them back. She became a Christian and started attending our church because it was around the corner from her house. She was loud and poor, and her kids were not used to church. At least one or two of them would get up during the church service and walk out the front side door—in and out, in and out. We became friends. We accepted each other. We helped her, and she helped us. She needed loans to pay her bills, rides to the doctor, and counsel about problems. I didn't make

a fuss when her seven-year-old dropped and broke a cup from my "good dishes" at the church Christmas dinner. Many times, when I was drowning in piles of laundry and oppressed by the pile of ironing, Joanne would notice and take the pile home and bring back nicely pressed shirts and dresses. She loved to iron! Such an encouragement to me. On my own, I would never have approached a tough, tattooed woman, but God saw fit to bring us together.

This is such an example to all of us. There are so many people who are different from us who we may totally enjoy if we gave them the chance. We just need to go out of our comfort zone and extend hospitality and grace.

In 2 Corinthians 8:7–8 Paul tells the church at Corinth that they abound in everything, faith, knowledge, diligence. He was encouraging Titus to make sure he collected money for the poor, and in verse 8 it reads,

> "I am not speaking this as a command, but as proving through the earnestness of others the sincerity of your love also."

So, he is saying that if you are giving to others, it should not be out of obligation but from the heart. From the

heart. I think that speaks volumes on what true compassion is for us. What is our motivation?

I think one of the most memorized passages in Scripture comes from Phil. 2:1–4. It perfectly fits this chapter.

> "Therefore if there is any encouragement in Christ, if there is any consolation of love, if there is any fellowship of the spirit, if any affection and compassion, make my joy complete by being of the same mind, maintaining the same love, united in spirit, intent on one purpose. Do nothing from selfishness or empty conceit but with humility of mind let each of you regard one another as more important than himself; do not merely look out for your interests, but also for the interests of others."

Finding the solution to motivate us to love each other and serve each other is tough, but I think if we can keep it on our radar, that is the first step. Pray about it even if you feel like you don't want to. Ask God to give you ideas of who needs you and what you should do to serve. Stay in the Word. I find great encouragement and guidance by reading my Bible. Reach out to meet others and spend time with your neighbors. It is not always easy, since our time is so precious to us. Maybe just make a commitment to take a meal or help someone once a month. If someone doesn't come to mind, ask to volunteer at the local shelter or food bank.

I love Galatians 6:9–10, which says,

> "Let us not lose heart in doing good, for in due time we shall reap if we do not grow weary. So then while we have opportunity, let us do good to all people, and especially to those who are of the household of the faith."

I have been over-extended a time or two (or three or four). I am very thankful for my husband and his desire to serve others because that has made it all the easier. And it is common to get tired and want to give up when things are crazy. These verses have often come to my mind. It is amazing that one day I can feel overwhelmed, and the next day feel like the sun is shining bright and feel blessed to my core and ready to bless others.

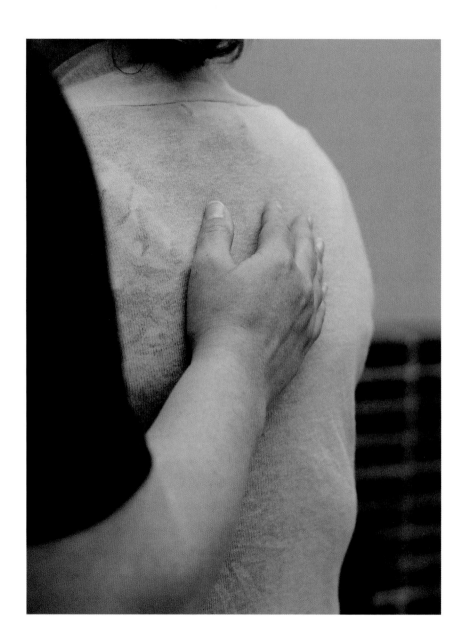

CHAPTER 21

The Samaritan in All of Us

"And who is my neighbor?"
—Luke 10:29

You may have heard since you were young children of the generous traveler who stopped to help the beaten man. Luke 10:30–37 is a perfect example of sacrificial giving of oneself. I sometimes heard it taught with the emphasis on the fact that the man was a Samaritan from Samaria, a land that was not well thought of in that time. The Samaritans were thought to be not only racially inferior, but spiritually inferior, especially by those in Jerusalem. The road was narrow and steep, and there were often robbers. It was not the best road to travel for anyone. As I got older and studied this passage, I saw that this passage has so much more to offer us. Let's take a deeper look at these very special verses to see what they have for us to learn about helping others.

If you look at Luke 10:25–29, you see that Jesus is talking to a lawyer who wanted to show Jesus that he was well versed in the Law. He tests Jesus with questions showing his righteousness. He says to Jesus, "Teacher, what shall I do to inherit eternal life?" Jesus answers in verse 26, "What is written in the law? What is your reading of it?" The lawyer gives Him his rote answer that he has memorized to show he is righteous. "You shall love the Lord your God with all you heart, with all your soul and with all your strength, and with all your mind, and your neighbor as yourself."

The lawyer continues, "And who is my neighbor?" In that time, it was thought that your neighbor was only someone who was righteous or someone just like you or me. The holy and righteous leaders in Jerusalem looked down on the downtrodden rather than caring for them.

Jesus responds with a parable of mercy in verses 30–37,

> "Jesus replied and said, 'a certain man was going down from Jerusalem to Jericho; and he fell among robbers and they stripped him and beat him, and went off leaving him half dead. And by chance a certain priest was going down on that road, and when he saw him he passed by on the other side. And likewise a Levite also, when he came to the place and saw him passed by on the other side. But a certain Samaritan, who was on a journey, came upon him; and when he saw him he felt compassion, and came to him and bandaged up his wounds, pouring oil and wine on them, and he put him on his own beast, and brought him to an inn and took care of him. And on the next day he took out two denarii and gave them to the innkeeper and said, 'Take care of him and whatever more you spend, when I return, I will repay you.' Which of these three do you think proved to be the neighbor to the man who fell into the robber's hands? And he said, 'The one who showed mercy toward him.' And Jesus said to him, "Go and do the same.""

I think about the priest and Levite passing by the wounded person dying by the road and the Samaritan stopping to help. He did not need to stop. As a matter of fact, he most likely would have been looked down upon. But he felt compassion. You know that feeling that tugs at your heart so you just can't let something go. It is a yearning inside you. This shows us mercy on so many levels. First, the fact that the Samaritan was at great risk to even travel that road. Then he stops to help someone and transport him back to the village.

He also gave up his medicine he traveled with and gave two days' wages to the innkeeper to care for the man. Would I sacrifice for a person dying on the street or pass it off to someone else? Jesus tells us to go and do likewise. Ok so that doesn't say to only help your friends or family. It instructs us to show mercy, care and concern to everyone.

It is a clear statement we are to help others. If there is any one main reason for this book, it is to encourage everyone—me included—to help those in need. So how do we do this? I pray for opportunities. It doesn't mean we ignore those close to us but it is far easier to help our loved ones. We need to find opportunities to reach further out of our comfort zone to those who are desperate. There are many more ways we can do this.

Cathy shares how different people reached out and helped her family in a time of need:

My granddaughter was born way too early and spent most of July, August, and part of September in the NICU (neonatal intensive care unit). After growing and developing at a good pace she was finally released to join her parents and brother at home. What a glorious, incredible day that was!

That relief was quickly replaced, however, by fear and dread when baby Ruby was diagnosed with Retinoblastoma, cancer on her retina. Our tiny baby girl's life was in jeopardy, and we were in an all-out battle to save her life. The long days of waiting that made up the NICU stay were replaced by sleepless days filled with much research and many trips to see Retinoblastoma specialists and go to Children's Hospital in Los Angeles.

Life was in upheaval mode and the one constant was the presence of love and friendship. That love manifested itself in fervent prayer and encouragement. Those days were dark but infused with light. The light came in the form of encouraging notes which included gift cards. Michael and Nellie were gifted many tanks of gas and lots of restaurant meals for days up at the hospital or to be used when simply too exhausted to think about meal preparation. People cleaned the house and cared for older brother, Rock.

Caring for others in times of great stress frequently involves taking whatever you can off of someone's plate so that they can stay focused on the pressing needs of life and survival. Michael and Nellie were blessed to be surrounded by close family and friends who could give them breaks, allow them to nap, relieve some of the financial burden, and offer encouragement in a multitude of ways. Chances are you know someone who is not so well supported, please take a moment to consider what practical way you can encourage them. Start with prayer, of course, then seek a practical way you can get involved.

When my daughter was going through a really rough time, she had many people come to bless her. She was a single mom living on an income barely above minimum wage. People jumped in to provide childcare for free. Groceries were left on the doorstep: no note, no thanks required—just gifted. There were multiple times people came to help fix things, help with yardwork, or just provide friendship. They were small things for the giver to gift, but they were big blessings to my daughter. It was such an overwhelming example of how the body of Christ could work seamlessly—with no questions asked and no payment needed—just to fulfill a need that is presented.

My friend Mallory is a police officer's wife. She has known that at any time, she could get a call that her husband has been injured. She got that call. She has done an amazing job helping her husband and continuing to work and run their household. She was so extremely thankful for so many people coming to help and encourage her husband, and she shares her story, and gestures of kindness that were vital to her husband's recovery.

My husband was hurt in the line of duty and shattered every bone in his ankle, his heel, and broke different parts of his fibula. We met with a surgeon a few days after to find out it was going to be a very long recovery. It also happened to be the worst winter our area had experienced in over thirty years. So, with a house, a husband who wasn't at all mobile, two puppies, a kitty, and being a business owner, I had a lot on my plate.

One day we were out of the house and got a call from someone from his department asking for the code to our garage. We kind of chuckled and gave it to him. When we came home our entire driveway, porch, and sidewalks were shoveled, and ice melt was all down. I remember thinking how dangerous it was for him to drive over to our house when the roads were so icy, and how grateful I was for him to come, get the shovel, and spend an hour of his time to do something that needed to be done. We had a ton of meals and treats and notes dropped off just to let us know people were thinking of us. My mom would come over, clean my house, cook, and help with my husband while I was working.

I am a cosmetologist and the months of November and December are extremely crazy, so when my husband got hurt three weeks before Thanksgiving, it was the worst possible timing. Having family and friends help him while I was working fifteen-hour days was an amazing weight off my shoulders.

I bought a camera for my door so my husband didn't have to get up and "crutch" to the door. One morning at 2 a.m., I got an alert that someone was at my door. I looked and it was my brother and some of his employees shoveling my driveway and making sure it was something I didn't have to do before work. He made sure that was done for me all that time. I don't think he would have ever told me unless I saw it on my camera.

My husband had trimmed all our trees in our backyard a few days before he was hurt and was getting ready to take all the branches to the dump but didn't have the chance before his injury. I came home one night and one of my dad's friends had come over and gotten rid of all the branches and also had shoveled my roof off. This had to be done that year because of the amount of snow and ice we had gotten. It was a very dangerous job and I was so grateful to have him do that without me even mentioning it.

I think the most helpful thing was having people at my house all hours of the day hanging out with my husband and lifting his spirits. Sometimes I would come home and my brother would be hanging out and taking naps and chatting with him, or my dad would bring over ice cream and hang out, or my mom would take him to the movies to get him out of the house or take him on a drive. It was a long road of a two-year recovery, but we are so grateful for the help we had from people I never had to ask to help.

People who have something tragic happen like Mallory did, need immediate help. Or sometimes there is a death and errands have to be run, many people may need to be fed. In this case, it was a long time in which people needed to help.

We knew a woman who was sick for years, they could not find out what was wrong with her. She got sicker and sicker. For years, she needed help with her children and meals. It was not easy for those helping. They finally discovered she had Lyme disease. But it was years. Being a caretaker for someone is tough. It's exhausting, and sometimes those people need a reprieve, too. It is another way to help someone.

Keep your eyes open, folks: there are needs you can meet everywhere.

CHAPTER 22

Community

*"Our hospitality both reflects and participates in God's hospitality.
It depends on a disposition of love because, fundamentally, hospitality is simply love
in action. It has much more to do with the resources of a generous heart than with
sufficiency of food or space."*
—Christine D. Pohl

I had someone say to me a few years ago that there should be no poor people because they can just find work. This struck a nerve with me since I was in a situation when I was a child in which we had no income. My mom was older, so it was hard for her to get a job, and we were young teens. It was not easy to just go get a job. When they said this to me, I just kept thinking of these excerpts from Deuteronomy 15:7–11:

> "If there is a poor man with you, one of your brothers, in any of your towns in your land which the Lord your God is giving you, you shall not harden your heart, nor close your hand from your poor brother; but you shall freely open your hand to him, and shall generously lend him sufficient for his need in whatever he lacks. Beware, lest there is a base thought in your heart …. You shall generously give to him and your heart shall not be grieved when you give to him, because for this thing the Lord your God will bless you in all your work and in all your undertakings. For the poor will never cease to be in the land; therefore I command you, saying, You shall freely open your hand to your brother, to your needy and poor in your land."

You may ask how this ties in with hospitality. I mean, isn't that just opening our home? Hospitality is a heart issue. It is *not* just about having a place to party. It takes in an entire realm of being welcoming. Remember our synonyms on the very first page? Neighborliness, warmth, kindness, generosity, and so on? It all ties in. Don't just welcome people you know to your home; reach out to others who may not have a home.

An easy way for you to give to someone in the community is through blessing bags for the homeless. Several years ago, our church gathered together to assemble items into large Ziploc bags. The idea was that you could carry these in your car and hand them to those you see in need. Since then, I have seen many people make up their own with varying items inside:

- water bottle
- coupons for free meals at shelters
- fast food gift card
- granola bars
- wet wipes
- hand sanitizer/soap
- washcloth
- hair tie
- mints
- toothbrush/paste
- feminine hygiene items

We have joined a group a couple times to get Christmas gifts for needy children. We couldn't do much individually, but as a coordinated group trying to help we were able to make a big difference for a bunch of kids. One example: Our ladies group did a sock drive for the rescue mission. Apparently, they don't ever get socks donated and need hundreds of pairs. It was *such* an easy thing to do, and it was so needed. Everyone doing a little can add up to a lot!

More great ways to be helpful would be to volunteer at a local shelter or rescue mission. They are always in need of help for various tasks. They often need people to help serve meals, sort donations in the warehouse, tutor kids who are staying with them, or just to

260

visit with those who are staying there and listen to their stories. You can also donate items or resources for projects that need to be done. Maybe you own a construction company and know they need a shed built or new flooring installed, and you could donate your time and energy for that project. Or maybe you do woodworking and know that you could build some shelves or hooks for their storage room. Plumbers could plumb, mechanics could fix cars, and lawyers could advise and advocate. Whatever you have been gifted with and resources you have been given can be used to serve others in your community.

Here are several verses to encourage us.

- Deuteronomy 10:18, "He executes justice for the orphan and the widow, and shows His love for the alien by giving him food and clothing."
- Exodus 22:22–23, "You shall not afflict any widow or orphan. If you afflict him at all, and if he does cry out to Me, I will surely hear his cry."
- Isaiah 1:17, "Learn to do good; seek justice, reprove the ruthless; defend the orphan, plead for the widow."

God's instructions to us are to love others, not ignore them. He wants us to reach out to refugees, widows, and orphans. I think the Isaiah passage tells us what we need to consider. "Learn to do good…." We can learn. We can start right now. We don't have to join some group or organization to see the needs around us. We just need to open our eyes. I bet we all—me included—could take out a piece of paper right now and make a list of at least a dozen people we know who could use some help this very week.

Afterword

"Spread love everywhere you go. Let no one ever come to you without leaving happier."
—Mother Teresa

I am sure you can think of dozens of people who have been helped by others just like I have in the writing of this book: so many scenarios, so many needs met, and so many blessings. So, what is our role to be? How can we move out of our comfort zone? I think this is one reason that it is important for us to share our stories. They can bless others and encourage them. Life can become overwhelming sometimes. We may see no way out of a situation. Reading about someone who also felt no one cared, but had someone meet their need, can help someone to see that there is compassion in the world.

We can always find someone to share our bounty with, whether it's food, or time, or love. I hope you were able to make the list from the previous chapter. We have so much to offer. And there are steps we can take to help us be more willing to open our home. Find those favorite recipes that are easy for you to share with others. Create a cozy area on your porch or a small room in your home to visit with someone if they came to your home unexpectedly. Start small by inviting just a couple of people over at first. When you're comfortable with that, invite six or so. You will see that it isn't as scary as you thought. It doesn't have to be fancy; you can even use paper plates. Your guests will be thrilled that you invited them over. I have talked to people who are sad they never get invited anywhere. People used to host others all the time. Dinner parties have become passé. We have become such a culture of "quiet nights at home" that we don't get together as much anymore. Kids used to run between houses until dark, neighbors borrowed from each other. People sat on their porch and visited as people walked by in the evenings. We may not be able to do that now, but by inviting a neighbor over for coffee, we have shown her that we are a listening ear. You will be the person she may go to if she's in need. She knows you care.

One of my very favorite passages in Scripture comes from Acts chapter 2: commonly known as "the ingathering." We read that people were taking their meals together daily and getting to know each other so well that they were genuine with each other. Others saw that generosity and love and wanted what they had. The passage reads,

> "And they were continually devoting themselves to the apostles' teaching and to fellowship, to the breaking of bread and to prayer. And everyone kept feeling a sense of awe; and many wonders and signs were taking place through the apostles. And all those who had believed were together, and had all things in common; and they began selling their property and possessions, and were sharing them with all, as anyone might have need. And day by day continuing with one mind in the temple, and breaking bread from house to house, they were taking their meals together with gladness and sincerity of heart, praising God, and having favor with all the people, and the Lord was adding to their number day by day those who were being saved." (Acts 2:42–47)

They took meals together daily. They *knew* each other and that love reflected God. Trust me, people will love that you cared about them enough to invite them into your home.

The other aspect of hospitality is to welcome those you don't actually know or that you can make feel loved, even if not in your home. This is the compassion side of the coin. This is even harder. Once again I think we can start with things that are easy.

My husband and I made cookie plates for neighbors this Christmas like we used to in our old neighborhood. Most of the neighbors were travelling and were not home, so we had a few extra plates. I certainly did not want to have so many cookies left. My daughter suggested to me to take them to the homeless group that usually hangs out in an area not too far from downtown. Craig and I drove down to hand them out. I can't forget an older woman beaming and telling us Merry Christmas. It was so easy that I could do it once a month.

And there is also the possibility that you may be the person lavished upon, and we need to be a gracious recipient. This is tough for most. I grew up in a needy home. My mom did not want to accept help from anyone. Sometimes we just need to say thank you. God may very well be teaching us about gratitude. I love to give but it is hard for me to receive. But this can also show us how we need to be careful in how we help someone. Bottom line in all we do. Be gracious. Give a smile. Be kind.

The love we show others, no matter if they are a friend, a family member, or a neighbor you just met, shows that we welcome them and it makes them feel at home. It is so important as we build a relationship with them. We also can show compassion to reach out to those around us. It really is *not* about the pie. It doesn't matter if we have the best house or fanciest food. What matters most is how they feel when they are in our home. And the number of opportunities to help someone are endless. We just need to be willing and open to what God brings across our path. It is a heart issue. "Put on a heart of compassion and kindness" (Colossians 3:12).

I hope you are inspired to begin today.

Recipe Index

THE *Team*

Jamie Hudson
—
Photographer

Craig White
—
Technical Assistant/Editing
Assistant/Marketing
Assistant

Jessica Everett
—
Executive
Assistant/Editing
Advisor/Marketing Advisor

Annie Mintz
—
Creative Assistant/
Photographer

Tori Loeffler
—
Social Media Assistant

Re Loeffler
—
Marketing
Assistant/Editing
Assistant

Nathan White
—
Website Administrator/
Technical Advisor

Amy Crist
Merchandise Coordinator/
Marketing Assistant
&
Ashley Taylor
Ministry Coordinator

Ruthanne Beddoe
—
Editing Assistant

Susan Greene
—
Creative Assistant/
Technical Assistant
&
Julie Jaddickan
Ministry Coordinator

Jessica Owinyo
—
Creative Coordinator/
Photographer/
Social Media Advisor

NOT PICTURED:

Courtney Jordan
—
Editing Assistant

Team 3:12

A few years ago, I attended a Christian writers' conference. I heard from several of the workshop leaders that you need to build a team. Being a new writer, I questioned that in my head: "Why would I need that?" In order to go to the conference, I had to have my daughter help get some of the forms and proposals done. My son did my website, and my husband printed different forms for me. I still wasn't aware that I actually had already started to build my team. Then I was accepted by a publisher, and this journey began quickly. Then I needed other people to help with edits, social media, photos for covers, and bookmarks. I needed logos and posters. It was endless.

Now I have fifteen people on our team. They sacrifice their time and help when I am overwhelmed and have no idea what to do. I am so very thankful for them.

Our team is called 3:12 because our key verse comes from Colossians 3:12:

> So, as those who have been chosen of God, holy and beloved, put on a heart of compassion, kindness, humility, gentleness and patience.

col312ministries.com

🖥 nickicorinne.com

🐦 @nickicorinne

📷 @nickicwhite

f @nickicorinnewhite